Praise for
IoT Inc.

"Bruce is a great storyteller and is incredibly knowledgeable on the topic of IoT. This makes for a book that is an easy read, with lots of valuable information. It has something for everybody. Whether you are looking to just learn more about this fascinating topic, or if you are thinking of creating an IoT business, this book has it all, from developing an IoT strategy with great examples from many different industries, to building a business plan, to understanding your customers' desire for outcomes.

"Bruce explains how IoT is changing all industries, business fundamentals, and the relationship with your customers—it's about transforming data into useful, usable, and valuable information. Definitely a 'very good read.'"

—Tanja Rueckert, EVP LoB Digital Assets and IoT, SAP

"The world is awash in new books extolling the virtue of the Internet of Things (IoT) and touting useless numbers of connected devices—useless because it's irrelevant exactly how many devices are connected, but useful because just about anything can be connected. *IoT Inc.* starts by explaining what can be connected to the Internet—from clothes dryers to tires, from operating room monitoring systems to construction systems—but then focuses on how these connections give birth to new (outcome-oriented) business models for products and services. Disruptions will abound in industries from agriculture to home automation, from industrial production to healthcare, and *IoT Inc.* includes a way not just to recognize those disruptions, but to profit from them. Rather than focus on the technology, Sinclair focuses on the business opportunity, an opportunity that is ignored at your peril."

—Richard Mark Soley, PhD, Chairman and CEO,
  Object Management Group, and Executive Director,
  Industrial Internet Consortium

"Bruce Sinclair will help you *sell outcomes* and give you *a competitive advantage for achieving sustainable success*. In *IoT Inc.*, Bruce provides powerful insights on how and when to deploy IoT. Born from his real-world experience guiding small and large businesses on their IoT journey, the practical, differentiating tools Bruce provides are for anyone who is involved in selling physical products to consumers. If you are looking to develop an IoT strategy and bring that strategy to life in a way that sets you apart from your competition, *IoT Inc.* is a MUST read!"

—Joseph Michelli, *New York Times* #1 bestselling author
  of books like *Driven to Delight*, *Leading the Starbucks Way*,
  and *The New Gold Standard*

"I found *IoT Inc.* to be an excellent resource for all things IoT. Applicable to the tiniest of IoT, like wearables, all the way to the largest of IoT, like smart cities, this book will lead to better products and services for consumers and residents alike. This is not billed as a technical book, but it provides a solid foundation for every Internet of Things stakeholder—from coder to CTO."

—Miguel A. Gamiño Jr., CTO, New York City

"Internet of Things is quickly turning into creating an Internet of value in so many market segments and application areas. I enjoyed the simple no-nonsense approach taken by Bruce Sinclair in explaining IoT and its applicability throughout the book. Clear focus on creating compelling value for users and customers in every market area without getting distracted by all the hype and technical mumbo-jumbo needs to drive the evolution of IoT. This message reverberating in this book is exactly the right thing we need to shape the IoT-driven economy."

—Krishna Mikkilineni, Senior Vice President,
Engineering Operations & Information Technology, Honeywell

"During the past ten years I have worked with several IT and OT companies about the value proposition of the industrial Internet of Things. Clearly the value is for companies to make the transition from selling products to selling services to selling integrated solutions and finally to helping customers in transforming their outcomes. The Outcome Economy is the 10,000-foot, macroeconomic view of where the Internet of Things is taking us. Bruce Sinclair clearly explains how we will get there, starting from the ground up—from value creation and monetization to IoT technology and business models to ecosystems to outcomes. I highly recommend this book. No matter what industry you're in, it will help guide your strategy in this changing business climate."

—Prith Banerjee, Chief Technology Officer and EVP,
Schneider Electric

"The Internet of Things is not new or novel, but the business models it enables can be transformational. Bruce brings a rare business-value perspective to this catalytic technology trend, discussing the intersection of strategy, operations, and technology. Along the way he provides simple, principle-based, deployment guidelines and best practices."

—Ken Forster, Managing Director, Momenta Partners

IoT Inc.

How Your Company Can Use the
Internet of Things
to Win in the
Outcome Economy

Bruce Sinclair

Mc
Graw
Hill
Education

New York   Chicago   San Francisco   Athens
London   Madrid   Mexico City   Milan   New Delhi
Singapore   Sydney   Toronto

2 3 4 5 6 7 8 9   LCR   22 21 20 19 18 17

ISBN   978-1-260-02589-7
MHID   1-260-02589-6

e-ISBN   978-1-260-02590-3
e-MHID   1-260-02590-X

McGraw-Hill Education books are available at special quantity discounts to use as premiums and sales promotions or for use in corporate training programs. To contact a representative, please visit the Contact Us pages at www.mhprofessional.com.

To my wife, Jessica, who has always been by my side.

CONTENTS

PREFACE

WHAT IS THE INTERNET OF THINGS?

First things first. *Technically* speaking, the Internet of Things (IoT) is just an evolution of the Internet. No more, no less. But the business ramifications of IoT are revolutionary and will usher in the Outcome Economy. The buying and selling of outcomes will have profound effects on your industry, organization, and products.

It is for this reason that IoT is so hyped. Billions of sensors! Trillions of dollars! It's so hyped that it stands on top of the hype cycle (see Figure P.1) and even has its own hype cycle!

But despite the hype, the Internet of Things is real. This is best demonstrated by the size of the players battling it out to sell to today's relatively few IoT early adopters (see Figure P.2). I've spent a lot of my career crossing chasms, and this is generally the purview of the start-up. Start-ups are supposed to collect the arrows in their back while larger, more established competitors wait until markets mature and technologies settle. But not here. In addition to the high-risk start-ups, all the tech giants and many blue chips have already jumped into the market, brawling for a foothold into what is going to develop into the new business normal.

Figure P.1	The hype around IoT

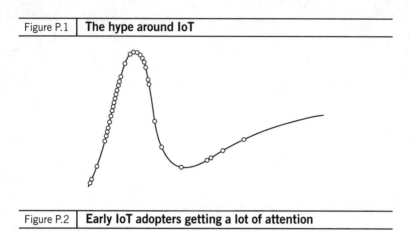

Figure P.2	Early IoT adopters getting a lot of attention

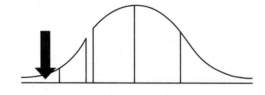

Some behemoths have already reorganized their P&Ls, drawing loops around businesses previously classified differently, to instantly turn themselves into IoT businesses. This may be a parlor trick to capitalize on the hype for the capital markets, but it also holds their leadership accountable to the street for their IoT business growth. Beyond that, some companies such as GE and PTC are all in—betting it all on the Internet of Things. This early and excessive competition, the accountability for growth, and the big bets on the Internet of Things are all testament to the business opportunity ahead.

EMBRACING THE INTERNET OF THINGS

If you're asking yourself if your company should embrace the Internet of Things, instead ask yourself if your company currently embraces the Internet. If the answer is yes, which it most likely is, then by definition your company must embrace the Internet of Things. It's not a question of *if*—it's a question of *when*.

Your investigation of the Internet of Things should begin now, but you already know that. By reading this book you have already started the journey, so the only question left is how much further to go.

The book has been honed over the last two years by the hundreds of business leaders I have taught this material to in my live workshops. It contains original concepts and has been influenced by the thought leaders I have interviewed for my podcast and video series on http://www.iot-inc.com. But most importantly it has been battle tested. This is the same material, same approach, I use in the trenches, advising companies big and small on how to plan their IoT businesses and product lines.

ACKNOWLEDGMENTS

This book began as a slide deck, honed by years of presentations in professional workshops around the world. I've been motivated by feedback from my students and the interesting use cases we've discussed. I've been educated and entertained by my podcast, video, and meetup guests, and I'm grateful to my consulting clients for supporting me while I wrote this book—and for making it real by letting me into their businesses.

I am thankful to the people in my book review club for their early interest in my book, for the time they devoted to reviewing their chapters, and for their encouragement along the way. Specifically, I'd like to thank Daryl Moon, Chris Drag, Shivanand Sawant, Daniel Elizalde, Paul Jauregui, Dale R. Smith, Reinier van den Biggelaar, Leena Manwani, Matthew Miller, Van Wray, Lars W. Kowalczyk, Ilya Pavlov, Matt Wopata, Mohan Iyer, Eli Richmond Hini, David Nordstedt, Gonzalo Escuder Bell, Matthew Balogh, George Brocklehurst, Mike Fahrion, Radomir Pistek, Ritu Bajpai, Catherine Dilan, Chris Mastrodonato, Olivier Gramaccia, Vishwesh Pai, Chris Herbst, Ovi Sandu, Jack Walls, Mazen Arawi, Patrick Dunfey, Farhaan Mohideen, Dan Yarmoluk, and Mike Gelhausen. I would also like to thank Jane Alcantara, who assisted me greatly during each phase of editing.

My deepest gratitude goes to my family: To my wife, Jessica, for her unwavering support, patience, and belief. To my children Paris and Chase, who learned important lessons from my writing experience as it unfolded in our household. And to my mother, Georgette, who has always been my biggest fan.

Last but certainly not least, thank you to my readers, listeners, and viewers, for whom I'm motivated to do my very best.

WHAT'S THE DEAL WITH IOT?

The five of us, maybe six, listened intently, and one took notes as Pat Dronski of Dronski Pest Control was holding court. He gestured to the floor of the small utility trailer we were in, explaining that mice traveled along walls. And except for in garbage areas, he positioned his bait traps on the perimeter of the first floor of each hospital building at University Hospital, which was his client. Pat's wife, Nicole, was a nurse there since the hospital opened 30 years earlier. Since then it had grown from a single building into a sprawling complex and in the process became Dronski's biggest account.

BUILDING A BETTER MOUSETRAP

Today Pat uses a product that hasn't fundamentally changed in thousands of years. Bait the trap with tasty food, wait for it, . . . and close the door behind, trapping the animal inside. Pretty simple and pretty effective, but we had a better way. We were literally building a better mousetrap with the Internet of Things (IoT).

Pat's office was parked behind his apartment building on Staten Island, New York. Hurricane Sandy had flooded his brick-and-mortar office a couple of years earlier, so he set up camp close to home and grew to like it that way. Generally, it was plenty big enough for him, his son, and his dog, but today it was a little cramped, as our entire product validation team squeezed in to hear what Pat had to say.

ACME Pest, my client, was in the early stages of building its IoT product, and we were visiting end users like Dronski to validate our initial ideas. Besides me, the team included ACME's head of sales, its regional manager, and Jeromy and Jordan—the grandsons of ACME Pest's founder who were now running the show. Our team, along with Pat and his not so bright French bulldog, Rocky, and the topic made for one of my most memorable product validation meetings to date, and I've been doing them for 20 years. This was day two of a five-day road trip, traveling together in a van visiting two prospects a day to validate our IoT mousetrap. I'll revisit a couple of other validation meetings later in this book.

ACME Pest was founded 50 years earlier by a Hungarian chemist who discovered that the wallpaper paste he invented had a propensity to stick to any mouse that came too close. Like any good entrepreneur, he saw an opportunity and pivoted, moving his family and business to the Bronx, where his company still stands today. His son grew the business tremendously by expanding into commercial pest control. His grandsons, Jeromy and Jordan, who had read about IoT, were convinced it was the way to put their own mark on the business and move their company into the digital age. As part of their homework, they attended Internet of Things World, where they were students in my workshop. After liking what they learned, they hired me to advise ACME Pest on how to best leverage IoT for their business and for a new product line.

Their distribution chain includes big pest control distributors, which sell their traps to pest control companies (like Dronski Pest Control), which sell their services to their clients, such as hospitals. IoT is going to turn the pest control industry upside down and along with it all businesses within each layer of its distribution network. Later in this book we will discuss how IoT enables ecosystems and the profound effect they will have on ACME's industry, competition, and products.

THE SILICON VALLEY IS COMING

Like the pest control business, your business, your channel, and your industry are also going to experience major changes. Your company may be headquartered thousands of miles away from where I live in the Silicon Valley, but whether you like it or not, the Silicon Valley, with its data-driven culture, is coming to you.

WILL THE INTERNET OF THINGS AFFECT YOU?

As the Internet extends its reach into physical objects and becomes the Internet of Things, it will rewire every industry in its path. What's considered a futuristic product today will soon become commonplace. IoT will become an integral part of every enterprise and every consumer, commercial, industrial, and infrastructure product. The Internet of Things will be as transformative to business as the Internet was, and if you stop and look, we are already witnessing the beginning of these changes all around us.

Consumer IoT

Our homes have gone from dumb to automated to smart, blending together security, energy management, and convenience. Inside, they are being furnished with connected products, from toothbrushes to appliances to beds. On our bodies, we wear a new category of IoT products, quantifying ourselves and our environment. And our cars are becoming more autonomous and better drivers than we are, an achievement estimated to eventually save 30,000 lives per year in the United States alone.

Commercial IoT

Commercial industries such as transportation are improving fleet management with telematics. In healthcare, IoT is augmenting the knowledge and skills of our doctors and empowering their patients with the information they need to manage or prevent disease. And insurance is measuring human behavior and predicting machine behavior to better assess the cost of risk. Everywhere you look, equipment is being instrumented to relay data to its owners to improve their business and customer relationships.

Industrial IoT

Industry is undergoing its next revolution. The Internet of Things enables manufacturing to produce better products and crank out more cars, more machines, and more chemicals for a lower cost. The oil and gas industries analyze sensor data to more efficiently extract, process, and deliver their products. Mining is increasing yield and safety with autonomous equipment that operates 24 hours a day. And agriculture is using yield modeling augmented by machine learning to increase output by using data from crop sensors and environmental data services found on the Internet.

Infrastructure IoT

Infrastructure is becoming smarter, starting with smart cities connecting their assets with their inhabitants and the vehicles in which they are transported. Utilities are distributing electricity more efficiently and more reliably with mathematical models simulating smart power stations connected to smart grids connected to smart meters in our smart homes that house our smart appliances inside.

WHO IS THIS BOOK FOR?

This book is for managers who work for brands and manufacturers that make things—physical products sold to businesses or consumers. It is for managers in enterprises looking to bring the Internet of Things into their organizations to improve their competitiveness. It is for entrepreneurs and their start-up's investors building a better mousetrap or inventing something completely new. It is also for those who work for vendors and service providers who need to understand IoT to effectively advise and work with their business clients.

Every IoT initiative in every company I've worked with starts with someone raising a hand and offering to look into IoT further. This hand can come from any part of the organization. Sometimes the IoT initiative is started by business; sometimes it's started by engineering.

This book is for those who raised their hand first. For business managers planning their company's strategy. For product managers and engineers wanting to make better products. And for sales and marketing people who recognize that IoT tech can help establish more meaningful business relationships with their customers. If you've already started your IoT journey, this book will be a valuable resource no matter how far you've already traveled.

WHY YOU NEED TO READ IT

IoT's Killer App

The Internet of Things is happening with or without you. And not because it's a cool technology . . . customers don't care about the tech at all. IoT is happening because of what it enables. The Internet of Things' killer app is outcomes. It's outcomes that customers ultimately want. They don't even care about products; they care about what products do for them.

Product fetishes aside, most consumers don't want to own cars; they want to get from one place to another, fast and safe. This has led to driving-as-a-service businesses like Uber and sharing economy businesses like Zipcar, both of which will eventually use IoT-powered driverless cars.

It's no different in business. Hospitals don't want to own surgical instruments; they want to perform surgeries safely, economically, and in the shortest amount of time. Mining companies don't want to own heavy equipment; they want to extract natural resources from the earth for the least amount of cost. Utility companies don't want the capital expenditure headaches of smart grids; they want to deliver electricity to their customers in a reliable and efficient way. And people don't want to own mousetraps, and certainly not what's inside; they want a pest-free environment.

The Outcome Economy Is Here

While operating behind the scenes, the Internet of Things is enabling two major trends that are shifting business from a product- and service-based economy to an Outcome Economy. Over time, products will be orchestrated to work together to jointly deliver the outcomes that customers desire. In parallel, the business model of the seller will align to match the business model of the buyer.

These two trends are brought together technically by the IoT platform. The IoT ecosystem monetizes all the technology involved by selling outcomes. Managers need to read this book to learn how these IoT-enabled outcomes will change their industry, business, and relationship with their customers. Most importantly, they will learn how to use IoT in their products and services to create incremental value, and about the business models used in IoT to monetized that value for profit.

Timing Is Everything

The Internet of Things is coming fast and isn't waiting for anyone. The challenge is to predict when it will arrive in your industry and when you should release your IoT product.

Timing is everything, and IoT is no exception; in fact, it's of even more consequence. Why? Because IoT years are like dog years, and being even a little late to this party can have devastating, Kodaklike consequences. Let me explain.

IoT enables you to perfect your product faster. Today, with traditional physical products, understanding what your customer wants requires customer visits, taking time and resources. Then, realizing those needs in your product takes even longer. The turnaround time to release a new manufactured product can take up to a year. IoT dramatically shortens the release process. It provides a 24/7 window into your customers' business, clearly telling you what they do with your product, how they use your product, and, most importantly, how they make money with your product. This, coupled with IoT's ability to update your product remotely with software, enables IoT companies to release new versions of their product at least seven times faster than traditional companies (my unscientific calculation). So having a competitor hit the market with an IoT product one year before yours gives that competitor the advantages of a seven-year head start.

Traditional Companies Will Be Left Behind

Enterprises that fail to enter their market at the right time with an IoT offering will face strong headwinds, and stragglers won't be able to catch up, making their offering obsolete. But there's more here than just a footrace. IoT changes how companies compete and in the process changes the playing field in ways that are not obvious today. It can shift the boundaries of competition, disintermediate the weak, subsume conventional product categories, and change business models into the most important feature of all. Sound far-fetched? Imagine the difference in market intelligence between Uber and the traditional "yellow cab" company. Perhaps 10 times, 100 times? That's the leverage to be had from getting out first with an IoT product.

THE TAKEAWAY

After reading this book, managers will be able to develop their IoT strategy and produce their company's IoT business plan.

BOOK OVERVIEW

This book is organized into three parts. Part One explains the fundamentals of creating and monetizing IoT value. Part Two helps readers develop and then execute their IoT strategy. And Part Three dives into IoT technology. But the tech is never that far away.

The challenge of explaining IoT comes from the breadth and depth of not only its technology, but in this case the different applications of its technology in business. But a point of view must be taken, and the one I chose for this book is the "buy-and-sell" perspective. That is, buy IoT technology, integrate it into your product, and sell it to your customers. This product can be a discrete product such as consumer goods, commercial equipment, or industrial machinery, or it can as easily be a system or environment, such as telematics or smart cities.

If that isn't broad enough, the lessons learned in this book are also applicable to the "buy-and-use" perspective. That is, buy an IoT product, integrate it into your operations, and then use it within your company.

Part One

Part One starts by defining IoT. It digs down a layer below today's pop narrative to describe the tech we're dealing with. More than that, though, it views the technical components of IoT from a value perspective. This business view of the technology will be a cornerstone for the rest of the book.

Then without fluff or fanfare, the book gets to the core of business: value generation and monetization. It answers the questions, in what ways can we use IoT to create incremental value and what are the classes of business models we can choose from to make money? IoT tech and the business models to monetize it are intrinsically linked. You will discover that as the technology advances, so too will the business model—increasing in strategic importance until it becomes the IoT product's most strategic feature.

One of the most profound benefits of using IoT properly is the unprecedented view we get into our customer's business. We will discuss how that can translate into a deeper and more profitable relationship for both parties involved.

Part Two

Part Two establishes an IoT lens through which to look at your customers, your industry, and your competition to develop your business strategy. Leveraging IoT's unique data capabilities to focus on outcomes, rather than products and services, will transform your industry and competitive space.

With this background the book dissects the Outcome Economy: what it is, how to become part of it, and why it will become important to business.

To effectively build, sell, and support an IoT product, the enterprise must become data driven—the ethos of the Silicon Valley. Internet of Things companies will use data to develop and sell products more effectively, support customers more effectively, and partner more effectively. This book describes how to become an IoT company on a department-by-department basis. To compete using the Internet of Things, new intellectual property must be developed. First and foremost, software development and data science must to be spliced into every traditional company's DNA to best leverage its institutional and domain knowledge in the future.

Next the book develops the concept of value modeling—a unique approach to qualify and then quantify the IoT product's value proposition. This leads directly to a top-down methodology to define the requirements of your IoT product. IoT is unique in that we consider more than just customer requirements.

Part Two finishes with advice on how to start your new IoT initiative. Although new theory is presented in the book, all concepts have been battlefield tested—practiced in the real world by my clients in developing their IoT businesses and product lines.

Part Three

Part Three demands that you put on your gum boots to wade into the bits of IoT tech in all its grandeur. And it covers it all: software, hardware, networking, data, analytics, and security. Not deep enough to implement it, but certainly deep enough to enable you to have meaningful discussions with your engineering team. This comes from the confidence gained by knowing how IoT works and, more importantly, understanding the benefits it can bring to your business and your customers.

Each industry is going to transition to the Outcome Economy at its own pace. Your job, since you raised your hand, is to plan your IoT business and to propose when the time is right to begin. This starts with the fundamentals, so let's get to it.

Chapter 1 starts things off by dissecting IoT tech from a value perspective. Let's go.

PART ONE

THE BUSINESS END OF IOT

The essence of any business is selling something of value to your customers. This boils down to value creation and monetization. In this first part of the book, we examine the different ways to use IoT technology to create value—fundamentals applicable to any business. We then look at the business model classes used to monetize that value. These ways of selling products are not necessarily unique to IoT, but what is unique is that we can measure them in ways that are meaningful and useful to the customer. By being able to measure our business model and our customer's business model, we can naturally align our businesses, and in doing so, we can change the relationship with our customers.

This is what we cover in Part One of the book: how to use the technology of the Internet of Things to create value and monetize it, sandwiched by first examining the technology from a value perspective and concluding with how IoT can lead to the best possible relationship with our customers.

IOT TECH DEFINED FROM A VALUE PERSPECTIVE

The Internet of Things is a technology you can use in your product and your company to greatly increase value and competitiveness. Since it's new, we need to understand how it works before we can put it to work. Right now, it may seem futuristic, but it's not. It's being used today to make money—and how it works is not complicated, at least not for our purposes.

Let's start with a few definitions. I'll be using the term *Internet of Things product*, or *IoT product*, in this book. I don't like the term *connected product*, or *smart product*

TECH TALK

An IoT product can be:
1. A discrete product
2. A system
3. An environment

for that matter. I don't like them because I think they set the bar too low.

We've had smart products for over half a century. For a long time we've been using embedded systems to make dumb products smart—so nothing new here. And connected products are at least a decade old; I was using an iPhone 1 in 2008 to control devices and access sensors across the world to demonstrate my then company's connected home platform. It's for these reasons I use the term *IoT product*. The IoT product goes beyond the smart product and the connected product by bringing to bear the full capability of the Internet into physical products. Unfortunately the "IoT home" doesn't have the same recognition or ring to it as the "smart home" or "connected home," so I'll still use *smart* and *connected* as adjectives for certain types of products.

Having said that, an IoT product is actually a system, or more precisely, a system of systems. It's self-aware and communicates with other systems and people. In this book an IoT product is overloaded to mean a discrete product, or a closed system, or a closed environment. An example of an IoT product is a connected clothes dryer. An example of an IoT system is a telematics product for transportation logistics. And an example of an IoT environment is a smart building. In all cases, these are physical things . . . physical products.

The Internet of Things is still being standardized. As such, when developing an IoT product, the company often needs help "gluing" the different subsystems or components together. My clients employ one of two types of assembly partners to help their internal engineering team. When building systems or environments, like telematics or smart buildings, we work with system integrators. When building discrete products, like clothes dryers, we work with design houses. Reliance on these partners will decrease as IoT technology matures and standardizes.

Both types of service providers are new to IoT, and they naturally approach it based on their experience and institutional knowledge. System integrators approach IoT as they do networks. Design houses approach IoT as they do industrial design or mobile app development. And as expected, both view the technology behind IoT products differently.

THE SYSTEM INTEGRATOR VIEW

Engineers look at IoT technology as a networking stack, which is, in a sense, simply a protocol map (see Figure 1.1). Mapping protocols from where the sensor data come in, to the application is the absolute wrong way to look at the tech—at least for business. This is plumbing and not where the value originates. It does not mean that if you sell plumbing, you are not providing value, but plumbing is a means to an end; it is the way to get data from one place to another.

> **TECH TALK**
>
> A protocol is a language used to communicate between devices or systems. For details, see the section "Network Fabric" below.

I don't look at IoT tech as a networking stack because it doesn't properly isolate and highlight where value is created.

Figure 1.1	**Network engineer's view of IoT**

Engineer Stack

TCP/IP Model	IoT Applications
Data Format	Binary, JSON, CBOR
Application Layer	CoAP, MQTT, XMPP, DDS
Transport Layer	UDP
Internet Layer	IPv6/IP Routing
	6LoWPAN
Network/Link Layer	IEEE 802.15.4 MAC
	IEEE 802.15.4 PHY / Physical Radio

THE DESIGN HOUSE VIEW

Designers have a different view (see Figure 1.2). They ask, "What are the end-user touch points?" "What's the back-end interface for the customer?" And "How do we tailor the product to fit both their needs?" Designers look at IoT tech as a front end and back end with enabling infrastructure in between. That's a little better. That's a little closer to value, but there's a better way.

Figure 1.2	Designer's view of IoT

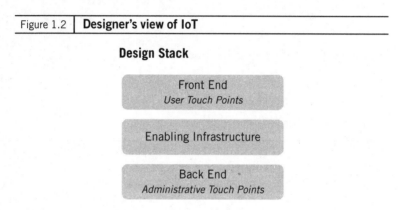

THE BUSINESS VIEW

Of course, system integrators and design houses need a business angle, but that's not their primary perspective. Inspired by cyber-physical systems and software-defined networks, the business view (see Figure 1.3) groups IoT tech into these four parts:

1. The software-defined product

2. The hardware-defined product

3. The external systems

which are all linked by:

4. The network fabric

| Figure 1.3 | **Manager's view of IoT** |

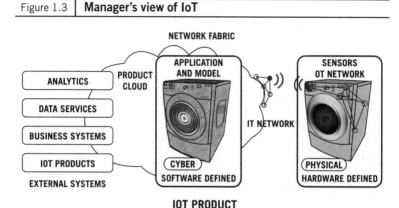

IOT PRODUCT

A fifth part, which isn't really a part, permeates the entire system. IoT cybersecurity is broader than IT security because it protects data at rest and data in motion, requiring knowledge in mobile security, network security, app security, web and cloud security, and system security. The business counterpart to cybersecurity is risk management.

> **TECH TALK**
>
> Cybersecurity is technology that protects the confidentiality, integrity, and accessibility of the IoT product's data at rest and in motion. See Chapter 16.

All incremental value from an IoT product comes from transforming its data into useful information. Information—IoT is pure information technology, and information is from where its value emanates.

The ingredients of this information are different data, lots of data from the product's sensors and external systems. The recipe, which defines how the data are put together, is described by the cybermodel. Value is created by executing the model with the application and interrogating it with analytics. This top-down view, where value defines the information we need, which defines the data we need, is the best way to look at IoT tech for business. The trio of value is the cybermodel, the application, and the analytics. All other technology is there to collect and deliver data. Let's use this value-centric perspective to look at IoT tech in more detail.

Software-Defined Product

The software-defined product is the star of the show because it's where value is generated. It consists of a cybermodel and application (see Figure 1.4), well actually many models and multiple applications. It may be helpful to think about this as the physical product's digital twin—the software that describes the product's IoT functionality. In a sports video game, the players on your team and the opposing team that are controlled by the game are software-defined players. Their cybermodels represent their individual personality and skills. The game application controls the I/O and executes the model in different situations and environments.

> **TECH TALK**
>
> The software-defined product consists of:
> 1. The cybermodel
> 2. The application
> See Chapter 11.

Figure 1.4 | **Software-defined product**

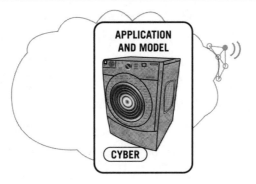

APPLICATION AND MODEL

CYBER

Cybermodels are software algorithms that represent IoT value and are shared by the application and analytics. Applications are software codes that provide product logic, orchestrate data collection, and interface with other apps, services, and people. The application executes the model, and the analytics uses data to build, compare, and solve the model.

The software-defined product and analytics generate all the value in an IoT product. As such, they must be the manager's priority, and they must drive all other tech choices. They also point to the internal know-how that needs to be cultivated by the manufacturer: software development and data science.

Hardware-Defined Product

Within the physical product, the hardware-defined product consists of sensors, actuators, and embedded systems (see Figure 1.5). Sensors are designed into the physical product or externally retrofitted in brownfield deployments. Connected sensors require an embedded system to convert the analog signal that comes from the sensor into a digital payload (data) and to send it over the network. The hardware-defined product's

> **TECH TALK**
>
> The hardware-defined product consists of:
> 1. Connected sensors
> 2. Connected actuators
> 3. Embedded systems
> See Chapter 12.

purpose is twofold: to collect sensor data and send the data to the application and analytics for processing, and to physically actuate the IoT product.

The hardware-defined product of the antilock braking system found in your car consists of sensors, an embedded system, and actuators: the sensors recognize when the brake is applied and if the wheel has stopped, the embedded system collects the data from

Figure 1.5	Hardware-defined product

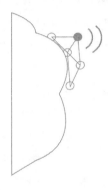 

SENSORS and EMBEDDED SYSTEM

PHYSICAL

the brake sensors and sends the data on to the brake network, and the actuators work the other way, applying the brakes based on the data they receive.

External Systems

The IoT product interfaces with external systems over the Internet to augment its functionality in much the same way online software does, connecting with analytics, external data services, business systems, and other IoT products (see Figure 1.6). These external systems provide external data to complement the internal data collected by the product's sensors.

Analytics is all about answering questions. It deciphers data from the past to answer, "What happened?" It processes streaming data in the present to answer, "What is happening?" And it makes predictions about the future to answer, "What's going to happen?"

TECH TALK

For more information on analytics, see Chapter 15. And for more information on external systems, see Chapter 14.

Figure 1.6	External systems

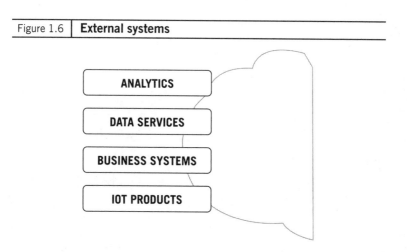

Functionally, analytics builds models, improves models, solves models, and makes comparisons between models and between models and data.

Internet data services, sometimes packaged as microservices, are tapped to provide raw data. Examples include weather, pricing, and inventory data.

IoT products interface with business systems such as CRM and PLM, as well as ERP and SCM, to exchange enterprise operational data.

Finally, IoT products are connected to other IoT products—extremely powerful sources of data and key to technically enabling outcomes.

NETWORK FABRIC

The network fabric stitches it all together (see Figure 1.7). It includes the OT (operational technology) and IT (information technology) network (also referred to as the fog network), the uplink, the public cloud (Internet), and private product clouds that

TECH TALK

For more information on the network fabric, see Chapter 13.

can reside "on prem," locally in the enterprise's network, or externally, most likely in a data center.

The OT network is the network within the IoT product that provides data to and from the sensors and actuators. The IT network is external to the IoT product. It connects to the OT network, often over the air by radio, and links it to the Internet via an uplink connection. Communication is enabled by protocols in the stack, which for IoT include the media layer (such as Bluetooth, Wi-Fi, 802.15.4, LPWA, cellular), the network layer (Internet protocol and proprietary OT protocols), and the application layer (such as MQTT, CoAP, DDS) that puts the collected data into context with metadata for the application.

| Figure 1.7 | **Network fabric** |

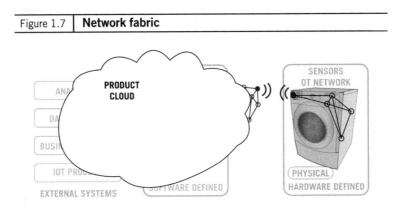

BRINGING IT TOGETHER

Generally, the narrative around the Internet of Things is about, well, the things. But that's missing the point; it's the tail wagging the dog. Value in IoT is created from the top down. The IoT value proposition defines the information needed, which identifies the data to be collected, which then, and only then, identify which tech and "things" are needed. Technically, the top of the top-down approach starts with the software-defined product and the analytics, which is fed data from the hardware-defined product and external systems, through the network fabric.

● ● ●

Before we define the tech, we must first define the value we want to create. In the next chapter we discuss the four ways that value is created with the data that are collected.

CHAPTER 2

CREATING VALUE WITH IOT

Value creation is at the heart of business. If an IoT product does not create enough incremental value, then no one is going to pay more for the product. That's a problem because IoT has loaded costs, both front-end and back-end costs that must be covered. Managers new to IoT assume connecting a product to the Internet creates value. They may be right, but it doesn't generally create enough extra value to cover its extra costs. The first key to winning with IoT in business is to create enough incremental value that it can be monetized at a profit. This chapter outlines the four ways to successfully create value with the Internet of Things.

MORE THAN CONNECTIVITY OR SMARTS

I've already stated my disclaimer in Chapter 1 about using the terms *smart product* and *connected product* as labels for the *IoT product*, but I'll use them here in their literal sense. The connected product is the class of products that use the Internet for their connectivity, so they can be externally accessed and controlled.

Consider the connected clothes dryer. It connects to your smartphone to send you notifications on the state of your laundry and to enable you to turn the machine on or off remotely. Are these command and control functions worth a 30 percent increase in price? What if there was a camera inside (often the next feature added)? Would it be worth it then? I say no. It's not enough. In most cases simply connecting a product does not produce enough incremental value to cover its incremental cost. Consumers expect this type of functionality to be part of contemporary high-end products. In most cases a connected product will fail. Just because we *can* connect a dryer, doesn't mean we *should* connect a dryer.

Value creation, as introduced in the first chapter, is not enabled by connectivity; it is enabled by models, applications, and analytics—what I call the trio of value.

The connected product epidemic is most widely observed in consumer IoT, spread by the false confidence gained by the less discriminatory money coming from crowdfunding. Of course there are going to be a few hundred customers for a connected water bottle, but unless it's priced very closely to its unconnected cousin, it's going to fail; it will fail because its incremental value doesn't justify its incremental price. Shop for almost any type of connected consumer product—water bottle, lock, thermostat—and the price is up to 10 times that of its traditional counterpart. The higher price is needed to cover the network infrastructure costs, but just because it's needed, doesn't mean that people are going to pay it.

The same challenge is faced in business IoT. Although there are more business models available to spread the costs, no IoT product can escape the need to create real, incremental value. The fact is, a connected product is not an IoT product, because as we will see in this chapter, value, real incremental value, does not originate just from connectivity; it originates from exploiting the full power of the Internet.

HOW TO CREATE VALUE WITH IOT

All incremental value of an IoT product is created by transforming its data into useful information. So how does this relate to the trinity of value: the model, application, and analytics? Well, models embody value, like a simulation, and they are developed by analyzing data. Value is created by the application by executing the model, and value is created by the analytics by interrogating the model to discover useful information. Now let's see how value creation is started.

> **TECH TALK**
>
> The models in IoT are created with statistics and used by the application and analytics. See Chapter 11.

Value Modeling

The first step in IoT value creation is value modeling. Value modeling describes incremental value qualitatively with a value proposition and quantitatively with a cybermodel. The value proposition describes the product worth, and the cybermodel codifies it and is used by the application and analytics to realize it. Next is to define the requirements of the model, application, and analytics. These are the product requirements the manager must be involved in, because once these requirements are defined, all the tech falls into place. You don't need to be a software or a hardware or even a data engineer to design IoT products; you need to be a value engineer.

THE WAYS TO CREATE VALUE IN IOT

In Chapter 1 we discussed the technology used to *enable* value. This chapter demonstrates *how* value is created and the *way* value is created. More specifically, it demonstrates how to do value modeling for each of the four ways value is created with IoT:

1. Make products better, with an example of innovation from commercial IoT.

2. Operate products better, with an example of how to increase operational efficiency from infrastructure IoT.

3. Support products better, with an example of how to increase asset utilization from industrial IoT.

4. Make new products . . . better, with an example of invention from consumer IoT.

Making products better creates value through innovation, and making new products . . . better, creates value through invention. Operating products better creates value by increasing operational efficiency, and servicing products better creates value by increasing asset utilization. These top-line and bottom-line improvements contribute to making our P&L better—everyone's ultimate business goal. And note, I will continue to overload the term *product* to mean physical product, system, or environment.

MAKE PRODUCTS BETTER

The first way to create value with the Internet of Things is to make products better.

There are many ways to make your product better. It can be made better by adding features comparable to your competitors'. It can be made better by improving its user experience. It can be made better by repairing defects. But the most consequential way of making your product better is through invention and innovation. A new or better way of doing something your customers find valuable is what makes products great, and in the process, it crushes competition, gains market share, and contributes in a big way to your company's P&L. These are the daydreams of product managers everywhere, and learning how to use IoT tech is a new and powerful way to achieve them.

Whereas operational efficiency and asset utilization, discussed in the next couple of sections, contribute to the bottom line of the P&L by saving the company money, innovation and invention contribute to the top line by making the company money. IoT allows us to innovate in ways impossible before, and increases in profit solve all problems.

In contrast to making huge leaps and bounds, the continuous improvement of your product is also important. Invention through usability, utility, and performance models will be discussed in the last section of this chapter ("Make New Products"). While effective for discovery, these models can also be used to make existing products better by creating feedback loops into design and engineering to understand how customers use your product and for what purpose. IoT also allows us to iterate on the product based on how it performs and provides us a way to upgrade the product to improve quality, add functionality, and fix bugs, by upgrading the software-defined product with an OTA (over-the-air) update mechanism.

> **TECH TALK**
>
> OTA is a mechanism to update an IoT product's software, usually over a wireless connection. See Chapter 11.

Let's now go through an example of how we can use innovation and continuous improvement to make a product better . . . in this case, a medical device.

Figure 2.1 | **Acetabular reamer**

If you haven't had your hip replaced, there's a good chance you know or know of someone who has. Arthroplasty is a common procedure performed on joints that wear out (see Figure 2.1). Hip arthroplasty is a 60- to 90-minute-long surgery that starts with a vertical incision through the skin over the hip joint. Once exposed, the joint connecting the leg (femur) to the body (pelvis) is dislocated and pulled apart. Once dislocated, the head of the femur is sawed off and a metal ball joint with a long spike is hammered lengthwise into the femur. Once the femur ball joint has been replaced, the next step in the surgery is to use a tool called the acetabular reamer to, as the name implies, ream out a semispherical hole in the pelvis to replace the natural joint socket. This is the tricky part. The hole created by the cheese grater–like drill bit must exactly fit the socket cup part of the artificial joint to be placed within.

Getting that good fit is hampered by a reaction called necrosis. In the same way that wood heats up around a hole that's being drilled, so too does bone. However, when bone cells heat up to over 131°F (55°C), they start to die, resulting in necrosis. If you have too many dead bone cells, the acetabular cup will not establish a good fit after being inserted, and over time it may move or rock with walking, creating great pain for the patient and great cost to undergo redress surgery to have the joint re-replaced.

It turns out that hip replacement surgery has a 1 percent per year redress rate. By the fifteenth year, 15 percent of patients need to be redressed. Looked at another way, artificial hips last for over 20 years on average, and the reason for 75 percent of those returns is joint socket movement caused by bone cells that were literally burned to death. We can use IoT to reduce burnout and redress surgery rates.

Value Proposition for the IoT Acetabular Reamer

The value proposition for the IoT acetabular reamer is *to perform the procedure in the shortest time while maintaining patient health* (see Figure 2.2). The key here is temperature. To create a better acetabular reamer with IoT, the IoT acetabular reamer will perform the boring part of the operation as quickly as possible <u>without</u> burning out the bone cells.

Figure 2.2	**Make products better**

Perform procedure in the shortest time while maintaining patient health
Model
- Temp = *f*(rotational speed, pressure, time)

Application
- Control rotational speed to limit temperature

Analytics
- Use models to predict patient results
- Analyze models for optimal blade designs and operating parameters

Model

Once we have identified the value proposition, the next step is to quantify it with a cybermodel. For the manager, models are high level—we'll leave it up to the engineers to code them into reality.

This model estimates temperature, which is related to reamer rotational speed, the pressure applied to the reamer, and the length of time the reamer is boring:

Temperature = f(rotational speed, pressure, time)

Rotational speed, pressure, and time are the variables (and data) required to be measured to eliminate necrosis. In this case the data for rotation and pressure come from sensors and time from a triggered timing circuit. From these data we build a temperature model to simulate how bone heats up during this procedure.

Application

After defining the model, we define the requirements for the application. It will use the model in different ways. The model is ultimately an equation, and as such, it can be manipulated and solved in different ways. We know what the max necrosis temperature is, 131°F. We cannot control how hard the surgeon pushes down on the tool or for how long he or she drills with it, but we can control the rotational speed of the reamer bit. This means we can reorganize the equation so that rotational speed is a function of temperature, pressure, and time and that it never goes over the speed that, when combined with the other variables, heats the bone cells over 131°.

Using the application to control (actuate) the IoT acetabular reamer means no matter how the surgeon uses the tool, the bone cells will never burn out, even if the reamer has to slow down to a stop. This also means that the application will speed up drilling, if possible, to shorten the time the tool is in use, and in doing so reduce the overall surgery time, saving money.

Analytics

Next we consider our analytics requirements. In all cases, we want to discover the causal relationship between the data corresponding to the variables we measure/capture for our model (cause) and the corresponding event (effect). There can be many models. In this case, one model could be associated with time to redress surgery and another could be tied to quality of health after a specified interval of time. In both these cases we would also want to include personal and demographic data such as sex, age, health, geography . . . in addition to the instrument's model variables. Predictive analytics can predict if a patient will need a second surgery or what the overall health of the patient will be in, say, five years.

> **TECH TALK**
>
> Predictive analytics asks, "What is going to happen?" See Chapter 15.

Diagnostic analytics can determine the optimal instrument operational parameters. To optimize reamer blade design, we would relate the density of the blade perforations, size of perforations, shape of perforations, and so on (cause) to the time to complete the reaming procedure (effect) to discover the optimal blade design.

> **TECH TALK**
>
> Diagnostic analytics discovers insights by looking into the past. See Chapter 15.

Value Generated

Although this Internet of Things product is used offline, it still uses the Internet to create its value. IoT innovation produces a new class of products that improve the effectiveness of the surgery while at the same time reducing surgery time, which saves the medical provider and insurer money.

Table 2.1 sums up the models, applications, and analytics requirements for the IoT acetabular reamer.

Table 2.1	Perform Hip Replacement in the Shortest Time While Maintaining Patient Health
Models	Model bone necrosis and reamer efficiency.
Applications	Execute transformed bone necrosis model to control rotational speed of the reamer.
Analytics	Prevent necrosis, reduce surgery time, reduce redress surgery, increase the quality of life, and determine optimal blade design.

Of course, we can use different models, applications, and analytics to create additional incremental value by operating the product better, by supporting the product better, and by creating new products based on the data collected, but I'll discuss these value creation methods individually in the next three examples.

OPERATE PRODUCTS BETTER

The second way to create value with the Internet of Things is to operate products better.

Increasing operational efficiency is widely recognized as one of the main benefits of IoT—and it is. Having squeezed out as much inefficiency as we could with IT, we now turn to IoT to squeeze out more. This is often the best starting point for an IoT product because it's easier to "sell." Since the other ways of creating value are less familiar to those approving budgets, operational efficiency is more likely to get a green light. Now let's consider the utility company's "product." IoT creates incremental value by operating the electric grid more efficiently.

Electric grids have been a feature of the landscape for more than 130 years (see Figure 2.3). During that time utility companies have been sending out field personnel to measure and monitor all components of the electric grid's power transmission and distribution

Figure 2.3	Smart grid

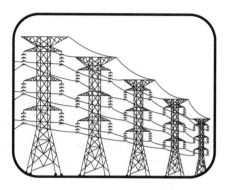

network. Readings are manually collected, from the power generating plant to transmission lines to substations to distribution lines to homes and businesses. Power outages are discovered only after angry customers complain. And when repair crews are dispatched, they have no idea what the cause of the problem is or where it is located.

Today, a minority of electric utilities use SCADA (supervisory control and data acquisition) to enable a limited form of connectivity between the power line sensors and central command. These smart grids (better classified as intraconnected grids) provide coarse data on the health of the grid, but most operations are still manually managed.

The IoT grid (my label) goes beyond smart and connected by instrumenting every node in the network to create living models. Once live, readings can be taken in real time at any point on the grid, from smart meters to transformers to substations and every wire in between. The grid can be actuated manually or automatically to perform tasks and to optimize its structure.

Value Proposition for the IoT Grid

The value proposition for the IoT grid is *to reduce operational costs and increase reliability* (see Figure 2.4). The key here is fluidity. To oper-

Figure 2.4	**Operate products better**

Reduce operational costs and increase reliability

Model
- Linear programming and network optimization
  f(sources, sinks, voltages between nodes)

Applications
- Remote operation of the grid
- Interface to highlight overloaded nodes to operator
- Close loop to develop autonomous system/process automation

Analytics
- Predict problems and prescribe fixes for operators
- Diagnose optimal energy flow for different conditions

ate the electric grid better means we need to have a higher degree of flexibility in order to react to market forces and the forces of nature.

Model

Our model will encompass three aspects of operational efficiency: reducing human resource costs, improving grid efficiency, and increasing reliability by reducing downtime. The electric grid, being a network of sources and sinks, can be accurately represented by linear algebra. The electric characteristics (voltage, amperage, . . .) at any point on the grid are a function of supply sources and destination sinks:

$$\text{Electricity} = f(\text{supply sources, destination sinks})$$

By sensing data at each node on the grid, we can build a directed graph of sources and sinks. This mathematical representation provides ultimate control, enabling us to change the magnitude and path of the electricity within the grid at any time with our application.

Application

Having this live model has profound effects on operational efficiency. The application monitors the model, displaying voltages (and other characteristics) at each node in the grid network, and highlights overloaded nodes. Data can also be sent in the other direction to actuate equipment, reducing operational costs by replacing truck rolls with remote control or by making operational visits more efficient.

Automation can be employed by using autonomous systems and AI to algorithmically manage repetitive tasks and work flows. And operational efficiency can be taken to the next level with human engineering. Energy supply and demand curves can be normalized by displaying pricing data to influence customers to reduce consumption when energy costs are high—saving money for both the consumer and the utility.

The grid is more resilient to external forces in its mathematical form. It is more malleable than a physical self. A hardwired grid cannot be changed without considerable effort, and like a fuse, parts can "blow," even if you can anticipate the cause. It is this rigidity in physical electric grids that causes them to "break," resulting in power outages and brownouts. A more sophisticated way to minimize outages is by enabling self-healing by making certain processes autonomous based on predefined rules. For example, if part of the network is getting overloaded in response to its physical environment, electricity can be automatically rerouted away from the affected areas based on linear programming constraints to optimize the system under these conditions. Over time, this AI can be improved by learning what works and what doesn't.

Analytics

Diagnostic analysis can be used to improve the model based on various weather conditions. Predictive analytics can go one step further to predict brownouts, preparing operators to dispatch service crews. Even more sophisticated grids will use prescriptive analytics to identify impending failures and then go one step further to actuate the system, rerouting electricity to preemptively avoid problems. For example, if there has been a history of brownouts caused by trees falling on power lines in a certain geography whenever the wind is above 20 mph coming from the west, we can recognize these conditions to predict when this is going to happen again and then algorithmically take the appropriate actions, in advance, to avoid the brownout before it happens.

TECH TALK

Prescriptive analytics makes predictions about the future and then modifies the product's parameters to change the future.

Value Generated

Value is generated by network optimization and remote operation. The IoT grid is optimized mathematically for different usage and weather conditions. It can be operated with a graphic user interface rather than sending out personnel with heavy equipment and tools. We can increase efficiency even more by allowing AI agents and other types of algorithms to take operational control under certain situations.

Table 2.2 sums up the requirements of the IoT grid's models, apps, and analytics for improving efficiency. This example solely focuses on creating value by operating the grid product more efficiently. We could also look at value creation from the perspective of making the grid better, maintaining the grid better, or creating related information products based on data collected from the grid.

Table 2.2	Reduce Operational Costs and Increase Reliability
Models	Reduce human costs, increase efficiency, and reduce downtime.
Applications	Display readings; actuate equipment manually and automatically.
Analytics	Minimize energy, accommodate for different weather conditions, and predict and prevent outages.

SUPPORT PRODUCTS BETTER

The third way to create value with the Internet of Things is to support products better. One of the first benefits that come to mind for anyone with at least a little familiarity with the industrial Internet of Things (IIoT) is preventive maintenance. Yes, it's true; preventive maintenance is important for supporting products better, but as we will see in this section, there are a lot more tools in this toolbox.

From a value perspective, better maintenance and support distills down to improving asset utilization—a subset of operational efficiency.

At 25 stories tall and two football fields long, the Bagger 293 holds the world record for being the largest land vehicle (see Figure 2.5). It is a bucket wheel excavator (BWE) used in strip mining and removes material equal in volume to 10 midsize cars per second, or put another way, it can excavate a hole the size of a football field, 100 feet deep, each and every day.

The Man Takraf, as it's also known, costs over $100 million, and like other BWEs, its uptime is only 41 to 60 percent, so there's a lot of room for maintenance and support improvement. It's current maintenance model is reactive and preventive. If something breaks, it's fixed; otherwise maintenance is performed on a predefined time schedule.

| Figure 2.5 | Bagger 293 bucket wheel escavator |

The IoT BWE creates incremental value with better maintenance, advancing the state of maintenance from reactive and preventive, to proactive, to predictive, and then to prescriptive.

An astonishing 200 million pounds of earth are lifted and carried away each day. This heavy payload affects the Bagger 293 in two main ways: joints break and the frame cracks—the two leading causes of unscheduled downtimes. Through an array of sensors, the IoT BWE measures heat and friction in its joints, and stress and strain on its frame.

Using sensors, and possibly actuators, IoT allows us to maintain products remotely. Without having to travel to the product, the service staff can diagnose problems, and in some cases, can configure the product or repair it remotely. If resources need to be physically deployed, the support call is made more efficient by sending the right crews with the right parts and by even hooking into the CRM to create a custom work order before the crews leave.

TECH TALK

Whereas a sensor measures the physical world and converts it into a digital signal, an actuator converts a digital signal into an action in the physical world.

Value Proposition for the IoT Bucket Wheel Excavator

The value proposition for the IoT BWE is *to increase uptime and eliminate unscheduled downtimes* (see Figure 2.6). The key here is to instrument the product to catch problems before they occur and repair them during scheduled maintenance times.

Figure 2.6 | **Maintains products better**

Increase uptime and eliminate unscheduled downtimes
Models
- Temp = *f*(load, angular velocity, vibration frequency)
- Friction = *f*(torque, temperature)
- Stress/strain = *f*(force 1, force 2, ... force *n*)

Applications
- Use rules engine to highlight if variables are outside norms
- Remotely actuate cooling or lubrication
- Remotely modify operating software to limit lift

Analytics
- Predict failures by interpreting model variables over time
- Prescribe changes to be actuated in the product to avoid future failures

Model

To identify the main problems associated with the IoT BWE's joints and frame, we will use three main models: one each for temperature, friction, and stress and strain.

With the first model, we calculate joint temperature as a function of the variables load, rotation, and vibration:

$$\text{Temp} = f(\text{load, angular velocity, vibration frequency})$$

Using sensors, we always measure the load, and then depending on the type of joint, we measure how fast it rotates or translates. These variables help us calculate joint temperature. The model's accuracy is improved over time by comparing the simulated temperature with the actual temperature of the joint.

The second model, also for joints, estimates joint friction as a function of torque and temperature:

$$Friction = f(torque, temperature)$$

We deduce friction by measuring how difficult it is to rotate the joint and how hot it is.

The third model measures stress and strains at problematic locations on its structure and builds a finite element model as a function of the individual forces:

$$Stress/strain = f(force\ 1, force\ 2, \ldots force\ n)$$

As in all cases, the variables in these models are measured with sensors.

Application

In the case of making "real-time" decisions, sometimes what is application rules engine or streaming analytics blurs. Independent of where the calculations are being done, in each of the three models, we are checking if the values of temperature, friction, and stress and strain are bracketed within their respective min and max values. For example, if the joint temperature is between 68° and 230°F (20° and 110°C), all is good; however, if it's over its max, the application actuates water jets to proactively maintain the joints by cooling them down. Similarly, if the friction in a joint is too high, we can close the loop and lubricate it. This so-called proactive maintenance attempts to deal with issues before they become a problem.

> **TECH TALK**
>
> A rules engine is often included as part of an AEP IoT platform, and stream analytics is often a separate product.

If the stress or strain of the structure is found to be too high, we can proactively issue an over-the-air software command to change the IoT BWE's behavior. After the update, no matter what the operators do, no matter how hard they dig in to grab surface material, the newly configured system limits the thrust and bucket wheel speed to lower the load

TECH TALK

"Close the loop" refers to the ability to actuate the product. The closed loop being product to logic and then back to product instead of a one-way communication.

and thus reduce the risk of cracking the structure. This allows the IoT BWE to continue to work, albeit in a lower capacity, until its structure is reinforced at the next scheduled maintenance.

Analytics

We can predict, using a subset of the variables, that a joint will eventually burn out or grind to a halt. This is classic predictive maintenance, the next step in support. This is realized with predictive analytics, which tries to recognize a failure signature in the data of the part in question. If recognized, it will predict that the part, in this case the joint, will fail. Of course, having accurate predictive maintenance is predicated on having a long enough history of failures of the same part to have a statistically relevant cause-and-effect model. Remember cause and effect. The variables of our value model are captured over time (cause) until there is a failure (effect) establishing a causal relationship between the time series of variables and the breakdown. Predictions are not limited to parts. Predictions can also be made about components, products, and systems.

Prescriptive maintenance uses different math to go one step further. Like predictive analytics, prescriptive analytics recognizes problems coming. And like proactive analytics, it reacts, in this case, to cool or lubricate the joint. At a high level, prescriptive analytics combines the two types of analytics together, anticipating the impending problem (predictive) and then reacting to it (proactive). Prescriptive analytics can be a temporary cure until the next scheduled maintenance or could prescribe a permanent fix to the problem altogether.

What's old is new again. Prognostic analytics uses yet another class of mathematics to more accurately predict the timing of something failing. If your operating environment is constrained and less fluid, this type of analytics offers many benefits.

Value Generated

This is the evolution of maintenance. We begin with being responsive: if something breaks, it is repaired (reactive analytics). Next, maintenance is scheduled at predefined points in time, say once a month (preventive analytics). Next, we measure potential failure points, and if we don't like what we see, we do something to tide the problem over until the next scheduled maintenance (proactive analytics). After that, we use data to predict which parts are going to fail, providing us the luxury of repairing the problem in advance of it happening and doing it on our own maintenance schedule (predictive analytics). And finally, we recognize the problems in advance and have the product self-heal, by using software or by actuating the physical environment (prescriptive analytics). Each step in the evolution of maintenance is progressively more valuable, with the last three steps made possible with IoT tech.

Reactive → Preventive → Proactive → Predictive → Prescriptive

The Evolution of Maintenance

The second trend is *where* the maintenance is performed. More is performed remotely through software commands, actuation, and software updates. If onsite support is required, personnel are better equipped by knowing what the problem is so they can arrive on the scene with the right parts and expertise.

The value generated adds up to better asset utilization.

Table 2.3 sums up the model, application, and analytics requirements to improve support by improving uptime and eliminating downtime. Like the other examples, we can also create value in the other ways too. For the IoT BWE we can also make the product better, operate the product better, and create new physical versions or informational products based on its data.

Table 2.3	Increase Uptime and Eliminate Unscheduled Downtimes
Models	Joint temperature, join friction, and structural stress and strain.
Applications	Tolerance checking, actuation for cooling, lubrication, and lift adjustment.
Analytics	Proactive maintenance, predictive maintenance, and prescriptive maintenance.

MAKE NEW PRODUCTS

The fourth way to create value with the Internet of Things is to make new products. Whereas innovation with IoT significantly improves existing products, invention with IoT creates entirely new products or product categories. By definition, this category of value creation is not just incremental; it has the potential to have a major impact on the company's prospects.

The quantified self product category is about measuring ourselves, our metabolic indicators, and the activities we perform (see Figure 2.7). And it turns out that quantification is big business—at over a billion dollars in revenue per year, with market leader Fitbit leading the way. Anecdotally, however, three-quarters of Fitbits

Figure 2.7	**Quantified self watch**

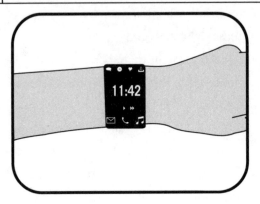

are relegated to the drawer after only nine months of use. Clearly there's room for improvement and maybe new products too.

This section is different in that we are making new products rather than innovating or improving something that already exists. Therefore the value generated is for the vendor instead of the customer—for the company that makes things, the physical products that are sold, in this case, to consumers (B2C). However, it may be bigger than that. As you will see, with IoT you will be surprised by the new opportunities that present themselves.

The tools of the trade here are the usability and utility models and various data mining techniques. With IoT you have a 24-hour-a-day, 7-day-a-week data view into the ways your customers interact with and use your product.

Usability models codify how your product is being used. Comparing this with its intended use can lead to insights into low-cost ways to produce product variability (new product models) through software upgrades, new features, or changes in the way features work. These models have been used to improve e-commerce sites for years, tracking how visitors navigate the website to achieve goals. For example, how many steps and what are the steps needed to buy a book? Different user interface designs score differently in achieving this goal, providing valuable insight to direct modifications. This powerful technique can now be applied to physical devices, but for the IoT product, this measurement extends beyond the user interface (UI) to the entire user experience (UX) in the physical world.

Utility models identify what your product is being used for, to be contrasted with your product's intended purpose. This can lead to insights that can be instrumental in the discovery of entirely new physical and information-based products. These models measure the functionality used, the environment in which your product is used, and other domain-specific variables. This requires the foresight to include sensors that not only serve the product's core purpose but gather data that could be tangentially useful to your customers or other markets. Extra sensors could measure geolocation, environmental conditions, the materials the product comes in contact with, and other domain-specific conditions.

> **TECH TALK**
>
> Product analytic models include:
> 1. Usability models that determine how the product is being used
> 2. Utility models that determine what the product is being used for
> 3. Performance models that determine how efficient the product is in completing its task

Value Proposition for the Iot Quantified Self Watch Vendor

The value proposition for the IoT quantified self watch vendor is *invention*. The key here is to use the data from one product to inspire new products—physical and digital. Let's look at a couple of examples that illustrate how to use usability and utility models with analytics—one simple and the other a little far-fetched.

Model

Each usability and utility model needs to be custom crafted for the product being measured. In the example of the IoT watch, we are interested in the way the interface is being used:

$$\text{Usability} = f(\text{UX}), \text{ where UX is the user experience}$$

And we're interested in how often each function is being used:

$$\text{Utility} = f(\text{features used})$$

Analytics

Our analytics will look across many IoT watches, plotted over time, to identify statistical patterns in interface and functionality usage. Other data captured by the IoT watch will also be combed for statistical relevance to discover what may be useful internally for our own products and what may be used externally to be sold as information products to new markets.

Value Generated

The potential value generated by inventing new products can't be overestimated. Gathering and processing data with IoT helps identify new product ideas that were invisible before.

Say you quantify the ways your customers use their quantified self product, in this case a sports watch—a watch that measures heart rate, cadence, speed, and location. Then say you discover, after comparing usability models (planned versus actual) and utility models (planned versus actual), that a majority of your customers are using the watch as a simple pedometer, repeatedly using the interface to get to how many steps they took in order to get to a "calorie burned" number each day. Based on these results, it would make sense to improve the current product's usability by making the pedometer functionality more accessible and easier to use. And it would also make sense to build and sell a new product, that is, a pedometer watch—a new product sure to have a market.

Another example, in this case to emphasize a point, comes from earthquake detection. I live in California, so I'm no stranger to being shaken awake in the middle of the night, which is exactly what happened the night of August 24, 2014. The U.S. Geological Survey (USGS) monitors and reports earthquakes. It maintains a network of seismological and geophysical sensors across the state, country, and world. The next morning we read the USGS news that yes indeed, it was an earthquake that woke up half my family the previous night at 3:20 a.m. With a magnitude of 6.0, the South Napa earthquake was the strongest to hit northern California in 25 years. A week later, however, Jawbone, which also makes a quantified self watch, released its own earthquake data. Since it measures the user's metabolic rate, it knows when people are sleeping and the quality of their sleep. It turns out that how quickly a person wakes up is a pretty good indicator of the magnitude and location of an earthquake. While the people at Jawbone could not precisely quantify the size of the earthquake, by analyzing their data they could identify the epicenter of the earthquake and its distribution pattern with more accuracy than the USGS. Now, I'm not saying that Jawbone should start selling an earthquake-locator watch, but what I am saying is that sometimes the utility of your product will have nothing to do with what the product was originally intended to do and will also be useful in other markets.

Beyond physical products, a new class of products is based purely on information and often sold as a service. These new products materialize from the so-called digital exhaust. Digital exhaust refers to the massive amounts of data coming from IoT product sensors. If your company is a data hoarder, that is, pays to transport and keep all its data, data mining this digital exhaust can uncover information valuable to customers in or outside your target market. In the case of quantified self data, it doesn't take much imagination to identify other markets that may be interested in human health data. Insurance and pharmaceutical companies come to mind, as do medical research facilities. Discovering value in your product's data exhaust may not be as obvious, but this does present an argument for keeping your data, at least for some pre-defined amount of time.

In these examples, invention is inspired by analyzing the data. You can analyze the data in specific ways to answer specific questions, and you can analyze the data to discover new and valuable information—information that can be used for your business or the business of others. Table 2.4 illustrates the requirements for creating new products using models and analytics.

Table 2.4	**Invention**
Models	Usability and utility.
Applications	N/A
Analytics	New product features, new product versions, and new product categories.

All the incremental value of an IoT product comes from transforming its data into useful information, and the four ways we can use this information to create value is to make products better, operate products better, support products better, and make new products . . . better.

• • •

Now that we know how to create value with IoT, the next question naturally is, how do we make money from it? The next chapter explains the unique ways we can use IoT to monetize value.

CHAPTER 3

MONETIZING IOT VALUE

Although we were only 18 miles away from Pat Dronski's trailer office in Staten Island, we might as well have been on a different planet. Confident Surroundings Pest Management was located on the twentieth floor of the fourth highest building in Lower Manhattan, not far from the World Trade Center. This was the seventh meeting of nine in our first-round market validation trip, where the ACME guys and I were getting feedback on our newly conceived IoT mousetrap from the top guns in pest control.

While waiting in what seemed like the lobby of a big four accounting firm, I read that Confident was the biggest bedbug extermination company in the United States. With over 250 employees, including 200 techs, the company dominated the hospitality and lodging pest control markets in New York City, which included high-rise residential buildings. After five minutes of admiring their accolades, we were shown into the company's Wall Street boardroom, where Paul Brass, the COO, and Roy Nery, the chief entomologist, were seated and waiting. Paul reminded me of Joe Pesci from *Goodfellas*—gold jewelry, a fat watch, and a $100 haircut.

Paul was all business and became noticeably engaged when we flipped to the business model slide of our presentation. While he needed to be seen as a trendsetter for his high-end clientele, he also needed to make the numbers work. And our proposed flat fee of $70 per station (IoT mousetrap) didn't work, no matter how much he wanted the latest and greatest gear. Confidence's business model was a monthly fee with add-ons for special services. He wanted to pay a monthly fee per trap, not a flat fee, even if the total he paid after a year was higher than if he had bought the trap in the first place. For Paul, our business model had to bend to fit his.

THE B2B IOT BUSINESS MODEL

Almost all the narrative around innovation in IoT is about technology, but IoT's data collection capabilities will have a profound effect upon business model innovation too. Using data for both value creation *and* monetization begins a new era in business innovation not possible until today. As IoT technology gets more sophisticated, not only does it provide more product value; it provides more business model value too.

A business model describes how a company makes money from the value it creates. In IoT, all incremental value comes from transforming data into useful information. These data, however, are not limited to what's useful for the product; they can also include information about the customer's business, which is in itself valuable. Today the business model is the seller's, but IoT will allow us to swap this to align the seller's business model with that of its customer.

This chapter predominantly describes IoT monetization for B2B, namely for commercial IoT, industrial IoT, and infrastructure IoT. Businesses have a P&L and need to profit. Consumer IoT is different. The value proposition isn't directed by profit— other motives are at hand here, which makes it more challenging.

The B2C IoT Business Model

The B2C IoT business model is a work in progress and will follow a different path from what's discussed in the rest of this chapter about B2B. Currently the de facto business model for the IoT consumer product is the same as that of the traditional consumer product—a one-and-done product purchase. The problem is, value and price are out of whack. A consumer product's IoT counterpart is much more expensive. At up to 10 times the price of a traditional product, the B2C IoT business model needs to change, and it looks like change is coming in at least a couple of different ways. One involves selling data, and the other involves selling services.

Advertisers, insurers, and any other company that sells to the same consumers are eager for the chance of getting their hands on the personally identifiable information (PII) of their target market. Selling this PII (with consent) is one way to offset the cost of the product to the customer.

The other way follows in the steps of one of the most sophisticated IoT devices out there—the smartphone. Similar to the handset business model, the price, or part of the price, of the IoT product could be amortized over the lifetime of a service contract purchased along with the product.

IoT products necessarily cost more because of the back-end infrastructure the consumer doesn't see. But nothing comes for free. To cover the IoT product's extra costs, consumers could end up paying with their privacy or for an additional service to make up the difference.

Business Model Alignment

If we sense the key variables of our customer's business model, we can align our business model with that of our customer. It's not the only factor, but I believe monetization friction—that is,

TECH TALK

An API is a set of commands that allows different software to talk to each other.

the drag associated with making a sale—is related to how aligned the buyer and seller business models are. Think of it as a friction coefficient. If the business models are completely different, the monetization friction is much higher than if the business models are related to each other—where it's just easier to get to a yes. If the business model of our IoT mousetrap didn't match Confidence's service business model, the friction would be too high to make the sale. Let's look at a few examples from Chapter 2 to see how this could work out.

The hospital is paid per surgery for hip replacement. Since the IoT acetabular reamer can count the surgeries it's used for, the manufacturer can also charge per surgery. The electric utility is paid per number of watts used. Since the IoT grid can track this, it too can charge by the watts used. In these examples, only the revenue contribution is being calculated, but IoT can also sense more of the customer's business model.

For example, in coal mining, revenue is related to the number of metric tons produced, so the bucket wheel excavator can measure its contribution by measuring the weight of the coal it extracts. On the costs side, it can also measure the variables associated with its operating costs, which include, but are not limited to, hours in operation, labor time, amount of lubricant used, parts replaced, maintenance performed, repairs performed, and fuel consumed—all measurable. When combined, these variables can populate a model that approximates the profit model attributed to the BWE. As the IoT platform progressively connects more of the coal mine's operation, from exploration to extraction to refining to shipping, a progressively more accurate, real-time model of the customer's business appears.

> **TECH TALK**
>
> The IoT platform is the middleware that comprises the technical underpinning to bring together multiple IoT products. For more information, see Chapter 13.

THE IOT BUSINESS MODEL CONTINUUM

IoT will enable business model innovation like never before, resulting in hundreds, even thousands, of different business models. But the usable ones, the valuable ones, will predominantly be permutations or variations of the five classes of business models covered here. These business models aren't necessarily new; it's more that they're now being made practical through IoT tech. They will also evolve serially from one to the next, with each successive business model providing more value than the one before.

Since the business model will evolve lockstep with the evolution of IoT technology, it's illustrative to plot the changes on the same timeline. This progression or evolution of business models is called the IoT Business Model Continuum (see Figure 3.1). The IoT Business Model Continuum is a useful tool for managers weighing their business model options. It provides a number of entry points and a directional vector for how they will change over time. This change in monetization should be considered as part of every company's IoT strategy. We start by selling a product and end by selling an outcome. Let's first examine these two bookends.

| Figure 3.1 | The IoT Business Model Continuum |

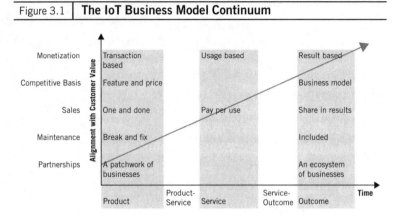

©IoT Inc. 2016. Do not distribute without explicit permission.

When you sell a product today, monetization is transaction based. There's a single purchase made based on features, at a price the customers internalize to calculate their own ROI. Although there can be ongoing support, generally it's simple—when it breaks, it's fixed. When buying products, the business customer needs to deal with multiple vendors and must both stitch together a pipeline to get the outcome desired and stitch together the various product ROIs to make a profitable business.

On the other end of the spectrum are outcomes. When you sell an outcome (e.g., a successful surgery, reliable and efficient power distribution, uptime for mining machinery), monetization is directly related to how well you deliver the result. Assuming you can deliver the outcome the customer wants, the basis for competition becomes the business model, and the sale is structured around the sharing of profits. Since the buyer's and the seller's objectives are aligned, support is included. Instead of partnering with multiple

TECH TALK

The ecosystem is the business counterpart to the IoT platform, bringing together the producers and consumers of IoT tech in order to monetize it.

vendors, the customer becomes part of an ecosystem that has the purpose of delivering a desired outcome.

The IoT Business Model Continuum goes from product, to product-service, to service, to service-outcome, and then to outcome. Let's go through each of the five classes of IoT business models using different IoT product examples to expose the nuances of each.

PRODUCT BUSINESS MODEL

The "one-and-done" sale is the safest place to start in your business model journey. The IoT product is sold like a traditional product; however, it uses IoT to augment its functionality and its future. Consider the Tesla Model S (see Figure 3.2). It is by definition an IoT car, and because of that it always has that new car smell. Let me explain. All Teslas have at least a 2G cellular connection to the Internet, and through this connection the company continuously improves the car by updating its onboard model and application. Picture yourself sliding into your car, as you do every morning,

Figure 3.2 | **The IoT car**

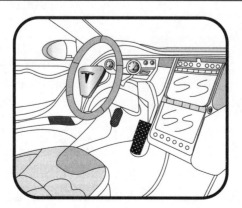

but on this particular morning you receive a message on the console informing you that the Summon feature is now available. That's just what happened with the release of Tesla version 7.1. In the fall of 2015, Tesla drivers woke up to a major, new capability accessible through their phone. That same day they could summon their car, and it would be waiting outside their office door at the end of the day.

Over-the-air (OTA) software updates can be used for other purposes too. Consider in early January 2014, the U.S. Traffic Safety Administration issued two recall notices, one for GM and one for Tesla, both related to fire hazards. GM had to recall 370,000 pickups into its dealers for repair, while Tesla quickly issued an OTA update to the 30,000 vehicles affected. The TSA accepted the Tesla fix and in the process redefined the meaning of a recall.

Besides OTA updates, your software-defined Tesla also uses advanced analytics. One way Tesla is using machine learning is to advance its autonomous driving tech. Taking a completely different approach than Google, Tesla improves its autopilot feature by using machine learning to codify the actions of its drivers anytime the drivers take over from the car's driving algorithm, presumably because the car didn't react properly. By analyzing driver "take-over" conditions and reactions, autopilot functionality is continuously improved. Contrast this to Google's approach of bottom-up development of autonomous driving without a human in the loop.

Business issues may be more challenging in your organization than technology, so releasing an IoT product does not mean you must change your business model at launch. Don't let sales and distribution issues mire down your IoT initiatives. A safe approach is to start with this known and established business model and then continue on the IoT Business Model Continuum as the timing makes sense (Figure 3.3). At the same time you are using IoT

| Figure 3.3 | **Examples on the IoT Business Model Continuum** |

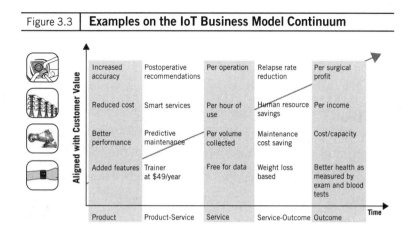

to create value, you can also use it to collect data to create information service products to eventually sell with the product-service business model discussed in the next section. This is Tesla's automobile strategy.

More Examples

Although this model is mostly today's business model, we can still produce extra value by capturing and providing extra data useful to the customer, either to be offered for free or, as discussed above, to be packaged to be sold in the future. For the hospital, the IoT acetabular reamer could capture variations in use by different surgeons performing the same surgery and correlate the variations to patient postsurgery health. For the IoT utility company, useful data to collect could be individual profitability on a consumer-by-consumer basis. Since the coal mining company is paid by weight, IoT BWE customers would be interested in how their percentage of shovel scoop filled, a key performance indicator (KPI), compares with industry standards. It's a little different when it comes to the B2C business models, but for the consumer wearing the

IoT quantified self watch for weight loss, calorie expenditure is something valuable that could be calculated and relayed on the fly.

PRODUCT-SERVICE BUSINESS MODEL

The product-service business model is a hybrid of the traditional product and the newer service business models. Adding an information service to a product based on its collected data is a great way to produce incremental revenue and potentially a competitive advantage. As we discussed in the last chapter, this new type of information product could be sold stand-alone and even sold to a completely different market.

This transition phase, between the product business model and the service business model, is a great time to start implementing the operational changes discussed in Chapter 8.

Continuing on our vehicle theme, the connected tire exemplifies this business model category nicely. Sensored truck and car tires are becoming the norm, especially for commercial fleet rubber (see Figure 3.4). Measuring temperature, number of rotations,

| Figure 3.4 | **The IoT tire** |

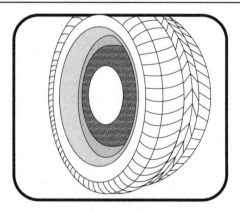

pressure, location on truck, wear, and height mismatches between tires, saves money. Major tire manufacturers are now selling tires with an optional tire management service to tire fleet managers. Tires are one of the top three expenses for fleets, up there with labor and fuel.

In the product-service business model, a physical product is sold with an optional information service product. This particular example revolves around vehicle safety, saving fuel and reducing tire expenses. Costly accidents, breakdowns, and liability payments can be avoided by monitoring temperature, tread depth, and the number one cause of catastrophic tire failure, low pressure. Underinflated tires also decrease fuel economy by 0.33 percent for each PSI under the recommended pressure. A quick calculation based on the 139 billion miles driven per year shows that this alone can save any major fleet millions of dollars.

Preventive maintenance dictates tires are to be changed after they have been driven a certain number of miles. This is an average based on average driving with an average load under average road conditions. Tire fleet managers put their drivers' safety first, but they also want to fully use these expendables before replacing them. By using a proactive maintenance system, the tire fleet managers are able to use sensor data to drive tire replacement, ensuring tires are safe but also not replaced prematurely.

Consider your situation—what type of information service can you add to your traditional product that provides incremental value and moves your business further along the IoT Business Model Continuum? This incremental revenue source could be used as a competitive advantage, or as we saw in the quantified self example in the last chapter, it could be sold into different markets. Think about the data collected by these tires. This is "out of the box," but if tire pressure change is correlated with location data, it provides a useful proxy to measure road conditions since potholes, for example, can be correlated with the spikes in tire pressure they cause. This information product could be of interest to municipal, state, and federal governments, or for that matter, to GPS-based mapping system companies.

More Examples

Let's go through our examples again to see what auxiliary data we can package and monetize to improve the customer's business.

A complementary information service for the IoT acetabular reamer could recommend the length of hospital stay to minimize long-term postoperative costs. By correlating patient demographics and health with KPIs with how the surgery went, the service could determine that having a patient stay in the hospital for an additional day would reduce the likelihood of complications that lead to the more complex and expensive redress surgery and hospital stay later.

By analyzing the correlation between weather patterns and failures, a predictive analytics service could be sold to IoT grid operators that suggests operational changes in grid configuration to minimize brownouts and identifies when and where to dispatch a ground crew, even before an outage event occurs.

With a 42 to 60 percent uptime, a predictive maintenance service for the IoT bucket wheel excavator would be very appealing. After collecting data on the same product for 12 to 18 months, you would have enough information to start making predictions about which parts will break down. Customers of this service would be given a list of parts to repair during each scheduled maintenance period in exchange for buying this service.

Once enough data have been captured, a smart strategy is to develop an information product and go back to all your customers to up-sell them on a new service. This is what Fitbit did after developing its new product called Trainer. For $49 per year, it will use analytics and your goals to become your personal trainer.

SERVICE BUSINESS MODEL

The service business model, or XaaS (anything as a service), is the business model often first comes to mind when discussing IoT, but it's not new. What is new is efficiently applying it to a wide range of physical products, including the basics such as food as a service (Instacart), shelter as a service (Airbnb), and transportation as a service (Uber). Rolls-Royce, however, was one of the earliest to apply it to physical products in a big way, with its jet engines (see Figure 3.5). Originally coined by jet engine maker Bristol Siddeley, the "power-by-the-hour" business model that Rolls-Royce uses for capital assets has been widely emulated. Rolls-Royce's insight was that companies don't want to own (and maintain) jet engines; they want propulsion for their planes. Trading a huge capital expenditure and maintenance burden for a recurring fee can make a lot of business sense.

Figure 3.5 | **The IoT jet engine**

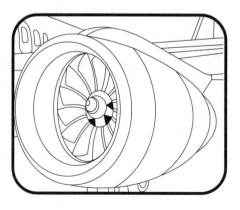

Rolls-Royce makes it even more compelling by relating that fee to the business model of the customer. And this is key to the service business model: to select a KPI that's aligned with your customer's business model. It could be units completed, volume processed, or, in this case, time used, which is related to miles flown—part of the KPI the airline industry lives and dies by: miles flown per filled passenger seat.

The service business model is not exclusively related to software or physical products; it can also monetize information products. Continuing with our jet engine theme, since engine manufacturers know the real-time fuel efficiency of their engines, if they collect other data, such as speed, altitude, bearing, and location, and correlate combinations of the data with fuel efficiency, they have something of value. For example, information services are being developed now that provide airlines a flight-by-flight report on the efficiency of their flight plans in comparison with the aggregate efficiency of similar flight plans by other airlines on the same route. Using this information service to adjust how to fly the four-times-per-day Seattle to Las Vegas flight can result in significant efficiencies. This is an example where incremental value is created by making a new information product with existing data.

Almost anything can be offered as a service. On a more light-hearted note, the Barcelona club Teatreneu started "Pay per Laugh—the first comedy shows where you only pay for what you consume." Using facial recognition software, Teatreneu charges audience members 0.30 euro for each laugh during the night, capping out at 24 euros (80 laughs). The new business model turned the club's business around by increasing the average ticket price by 6 euros and increasing customer satisfaction. This is now being copied by other theaters.

The service business model is seductive, but there are practical implementation issues around financing, sales, and systems that the vendor must be aware of. One of my clients sells IoT equipment to manufacturers. An issue we are dealing with is how to finance the services business model. Selling our product as a service is great for the customer, but it means we must fund the capital costs of the equipment. Our calculated 18-month internal ROI is great, but it still means we are cash flow negative with each customer for 18 months, putting an unplanned strain on our balance sheet. Second, we need to change our sales structure from a one-and-done discrete sales model to one where we must repeatedly sell our service every 12- or 24-month period. To achieve this, we must organize and compensate our channel in a completely different way. And lastly, we must deal with billing. Our financial systems are not set up to collect and account for monthly payments. Such billing systems are available, but they too must be financed.

More Examples

What is the main metric in your customer's business model? What are bonuses paid on? What contributes to people getting promoted? What is the KPI your customer lives and dies by? If you can measure it or measure a contributing factor to it, then there's a good chance your service business model will be successful.

Hospitals are paid per surgery. Therefore, it makes sense that the IoT acetabular reamer vendor charges by the surgery. With this business model the hospital does not need to concern itself with maintenance—it's included. And it is virtually guaranteed that the acetabular reamer will have that new car smell because it's in the vendor's best interest to update its software to provide the latest features and improvements in order to keep the customer happy enough to renew at the end of each service term.

For the IoT grid, the customer is paid by the kilowatt. Therefore, a per-kilowatt service charge will be appealing to the utility because it reduces risk.

In mining it's all about the weight extracted by the IoT bucket wheel excavator. The "by the metric ton of material extracted" service model is a win-win for the customer and the vendor. The customer only pays when the machine is up and generating revenue, and the vendor earns more by improving the product's operation efficiency. Of course, the only way to charge by the metric ton is by being able to weigh the coal and overspill (extra dirt) being extracted, bucket by bucket. This is something impossible to measure and improve upon with a conventional bucket wheel excavator, but manufacturers of IoT BWEs can include this requirement in their design.

Coming up with a service business model metric for a B2C product can be more challenging, but a good fallback position is using the KPI of time. How about the quantified self watch? Charge by the hour? Probably not, but by the month may be perfect for savvy consumers who want to test this new type of watch out. This works too for the watch vendor. After charging a slightly higher rental premium, the vendor can refurbish and update the returned watches and rent them for a second or third time at a slightly lower price—a better utilization of assets for all.

SERVICE-OUTCOME BUSINESS MODEL

China is the world leader in wind power generation, producing more capacity than the next largest producer, the United States, by a three-to-one margin. A guest speaker at my IoT business meetup in the Silicon Valley, from ParStream (later acquired by Cisco), recounted how his company's real-time analytics was used to improve the efficiency of a large turbine wind farm in northern China. Each turbine was analyzed and compared with respect to wind speed and power output. The turbine blade angles of lower-performing turbines were adjusted based on their better-performing neighbors, their spatial relationship to other turbines and weather conditions. While the technology was impressive, perhaps more impressive was the business model utilized by ParStream's system integrator.

In the service-outcome business model, the seller becomes a business partner. The seller provides the product or installs the equipment needed to improve the customer's business at the seller's expense. There are two parts to this business model. The first part is similar to the service model, but instead of a single product being monetized as a service, it's often one or more product lines that are monetized as a service. The second part shares in the upside. After a baseline is established, a percentage of the incremental revenue or incremental savings generated is paid out based on phases or milestones.

In the case of the wind farm (Figure 3.6), the cost per generated watt was measured to establish a baseline. A new cost per watt was measured quarterly. Based on the observed efficiency gain of 15 percent for the 20,000-turbine wind farm with 10-GW capac-

Figure 3.6	**The IoT wind farm**

ity, this resulted in tens of millions of dollars per year of economic benefits based on $40/MW-hour. The system integrator was well paid, and the wind farm customer was happy with the windfall—a true win-win situation with low risk for the customer.

More Examples

As we get closer to providing outcomes, it means IoT products are working together, first in product lines that operate together and then in networks of product lines that all operate together, both being monetized by IoT ecosystems. As discussed, the service-outcome business model has a service component plus an add-on payment based on saving or making more money that incentivizes the vendor to improve its customer's business.

In the case of hip replacement surgery, the IoT acetabular reamer will be connected to the oscillating saw and other equipment used in the operating room for monitoring, anesthesia, sterilization, etc., all gathering data for analysis. As the U.S healthcare industry is being transformed, a slow shift from paying per procedure to paying per outcome is happening. Insurance companies are now penalizing hospitals for unsuccessful surgeries, especially when redress surgeries are required. This new climate will increase the popularity of service-outcome business models. The add-on payment here would be related to the long-term health of the patient.

Human resources make up the majority of an electric grid's operational costs. So measuring HR costs as part of the revenue model, in addition to grid usage, is a good way to capture the operational efficiency of the IoT grid. This is a natural fit for an IoT grid that can be remotely operated and can automate many of the manual operations of the past. The add-on payment in this situation would be related to the reduction in human operating expenses.

After the maintenance costs of the IoT BWE are baselined, an outcome of lowering maintenance costs can be combined with the BWE-as-a-service business model. In this service-outcome business model, the vendor would receive a percentage of the maintenance cost savings relative to a baseline. The shift from preventive to proactive to predictive to prescriptive maintenance, enabled by analytics, will make this business model attractive to all parties involved.

Leading-edge auto insurers already reward good drivers, as measured by an IoT device plugged into the ODP port in the car, with lower rates (a negative cost-based service fee). Just as the quantified car insurance vendor can reward its owners with lower auto insurance rates, the healthcare insurer can reward the IoT quantified self watch owners with lower health insurance rates based on the amount of exercise they do. Okay, this may be a stretch, but it's a win-win that rewards both parties based on a common goal.

OUTCOME BUSINESS MODEL

Outcomes differ, but the king of business models pays out based on improving the P&L. To offer the last business model in the continuum, different products are orchestrated to achieve the customer's desired outcome. The customer's and vendor's businesses are aligned, and the risk is low for the customer. Technically, this is done with IoT platforms, but the bigger challenge is shaping the business. Partnering will become increasingly more important, and the partnering structure of this future will be defined by the ecosystem.

The IoT ecosystem is the business counterpart to the IoT platform. It brings together the producers (vendors) and the consumers (customers) of the IoT tech in order to monetize it. One or more ecosystems will be established in every industry vertical, and like musical chairs, vendors do not want to be left out. At a minimum, vendors need to be part of an ecosystem. At a maximum, vendors will found and control an ecosystem.

Let's face it—your customers don't really want your product; what they want is what it can do for them. Farmers, for example, don't want to own and maintain tractors; what they want is a bumper crop for a low cost. Smart farming is a vertical establishing early ecosystems (see Figure 3.7). At the forefront are vendors John Deere and AGCO. These competing ecosystems bring together farming machinery, seed management, irrigation, and weather data to sell farmers outcomes of higher crop yields at lower costs. Individually, each of these separate product categories provides value, but when linked, dependencies are codified, creating greater value than the sum of the parts. For example, what strain of seeds yields the best results for a particular geography, weather, and irrigation rate when planted, grown, and harvested by your brand

---

Figure 3.7 | **The IoT farming ecosystem**

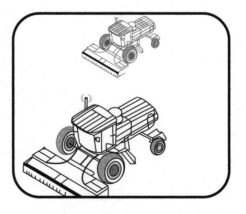

of farming equipment? And at what date should planting begin in order to maximize yield for your geography, weather, and irrigation rate? Transforming all the products into software or data enables them to be put to work in the best possible way. And the closer we get to providing a complete outcome-based solution, the closer we can align our business model with the business model of our customer.

As IoT platforms develop to encompass the product space for an industry segment, the service-outcome business model will give way to the pure outcome business model. The ecosystem shares the incremental cost savings or incremental revenue, and if both ends of the P&L are quantified, then the profit is shared. This goes beyond the service-outcome business model in that payment now is completely based on performance. This alignment of business models is only possible with a full ecosystem built upon a comprehensive IoT platform. This revenue model is seductive to the customer because it transfers risk to the vendor and completely aligns both parties' interests. It's attractive to the vendor because with the right technology and know-how, it can be very successful.

More Examples

For hip replacement surgery, an outcome business model based on lowering costs is more likely than one based on revenue or profit.

Unlike a surgical procedure, the smart grid is technically a contained system that could be monetized based on savings, increasing revenue, or profit.

For the outcome business model to work in the coal mining example, an ecosystem must develop that includes more stages of the mining operation. But since the price of commodities can change outside the control of the ecosystem, this particular example would be better aligned with costs rather than revenue or profit.

Like the surgery example, the quantified self outcome business model would have to be based on what is quantifiable, because human behavior certainly is not. This is a tough one, but sharing in insurance premium savings could make sense if customer health is measured and verified by medical exams and blood tests. This is starting to sound a lot like the Outcome Economy, which will be covered in Chapter 7.

This is the bleeding edge, and this business history is still being written. When jointly producing a solution, joint risk must be attributed and the thorny issue of intellectual property navigated. Like the service business model, the outcome business model must address new financing, sales, and system requirements. The outcome business model provider must finance the capital costs of the equipment, but it must also finance all other hard and soft costs. Sales is no longer selling a product or a service; it is selling a partnership, and once established, sales looks more like business consulting (see all organizational changes in Chapter 8). Billing systems that invoice based on outcomes are still under development, so today this is still a manual process.

The interbusiness models between ecosystem vendors are still evolving. As we are seeing with some of the leading players in the industrial Internet of Things, their ecosystem business models are mimicking the ecosystem business model employed by the mobile industry, where applications that "plug in" to the platforms are purchased and monetized à la carte.

At the end of the IoT Business Model Continuum customers will pay a single recurring product bill based on increased savings, increased revenue, or both, depending on the profits generated while delivering their outcomes. When this stage has been reached, when the ecosystem can deliver the outcomes the customer wants, the business model becomes the only feature of consequence.

THE BUSINESS MODEL AS THE FEATURE

We start with a product and then add a service to it to add more value. From here we offer more and more of the outcome that the customer is looking for, first by focusing on increasing efficiency or revenue for part of the customer's business and then by addressing the customer's entire business (see Figure 3.8). This process naturally brings together the business models of the vendor and customer.

To realize these business models, measure as much of your customer's business as possible by making it part of your product requirements. At first it may be only indirect measurements of some of the variables that make up the customer's revenue or costs. But over time, as IoT products turn into IoT product lines and product lines turn into networks of product lines from different vendors all orchestrated to deliver the customer outcome, more and more of the variables of the customer's business model will be exposed and available to capture. It's worth repeating: once we can deliver the outcomes the customer desires, individual product functionality becomes less important and the only feature of consequence becomes the business model.

| Figure 3.8 | **Monetizing IoT value** |

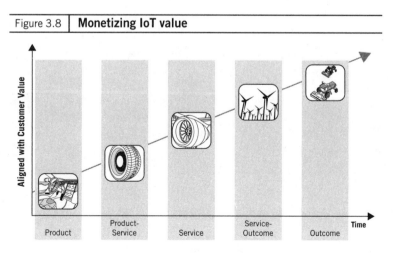

©IoT Inc. 2016. Do not distribute without explicit permission.

Although the concept of the business model as a feature is not new, it has, until now, been relatively obscure. IoT will push business models to the forefront as a mechanism of competition.

• • •

Perhaps the most profound effect on business is a closer alignment of the business interests of the vendor and the customer. This hallmark of the Outcome Economy pays dividends in value creation efficiency, but it affects more than that. As we will see in the next chapter, the entire relationship between customers and vendors changes . . . for the better.

CHAPTER 4

THE CHANGING CUSTOMER RELATIONSHIP

Although today we have social media signals to decipher, our relationship with the customer has remained largely the same over the past 20 or more years. IoT is about to change that relationship drastically.

If you choose to look, an IoT product provides a view into your customer's business. When looked at the right way, you can understand how the customer uses your product, what the customer uses your product for, how frequently your customer uses your product, where and for how long your customer used your product, and, ultimately, why your customer uses your product.

Sure, there have been less direct and more qualitative ways to do this in the past, but they weren't as effective. Product research had to be staged in focus groups or performed after the fact in surveys. It wasn't until the advent of networked software that vendors could get a real-time, real view into how their products (websites and services) were really used. Now by instrumenting products with sensors, IoT enables this perspective into anything you make.

I was a product manager and then the manager of product managers for many years—one of my favorite jobs. And my favorite activity was to visit customers. Visiting customers gave me new and pure data. Traveling to customer sites to see how they used my product in their business uncovered genuine insights into how the product should evolve. However, even as a young and unmarried product manager, it was impractical to spend more than a couple of weeks every couple of months out of the office in the field with sales—there were too many other things to do.

Consider how IoT changes this—it's a product manager's dream. The Internet of Things opens up a 24-hour-a-day, 7-day-a-week window into the customer's business. Furthermore, observations can be quantified into utility models (what the product is being used for and when), usability models (how the product is being used), and performance models (how efficient the product is). With this treasure trove of information, more time is spent analyzing the data instead of gathering the data. This doesn't eliminate the need to visit customers, but when customers are visited, the discussion is deeper and further along.

> **TECH TALK**
>
> A utility model is a simulation of how something works and behaves. See Chapter 11.

FROM CASUAL TO INTIMATE

In the past, most of the quality time spent with customers was during the courting phase of presales. Contact after the sale was sporadic, only meeting periodically during service engagements. With an IoT product the relationship is less superficial because support is continuous, and for clever companies, so is sales.

Through analytics, primary data can be interpreted about the customer's business and how it can be improved; this means learning about your customer's challenges and determining how they can be overcome. Through personal interaction with sales and service and through a more automated interaction with marketing, the relationship changes into being about jointly creating value. Once the product's data are quantified, the customer relationship is based on jointly achieving desired outcomes.

Each step we take through the business model continuum (see Chapter 3) brings our businesses closer together. When our success is dependent on the success of our customer, we care more and we care longer. We are more consultative, strategizing on how to improve our product and the customer's business—never selling, but selling all the time.

INCREASING CUSTOMER LIFETIME VALUE

As the IoT vendor continues to deliver value by aligning its product's utility, usability, and efficiency to the customer's needs, the lifetime value of the customer relationship naturally increases. With the ability to monitor each customer each day, the manufacturer compiles deep insights both in the aggregate and individually for each customer and is able to personalize the value proposition. A better product with a better value proposition is of course important, but ultimately it is the consultative business relationship that is going to increase the lifetime value of the customer by naturally increasing loyalty and hardening that relationship against the overtures of competitors, leading to less churn.

Increasing the lifetime value of the customer provides P&L flexibility. The increased acquisition cost and the cost of sale for this kind of customer are offset in time by more overall revenue. When the lifetime value of each customer increases, the P&L becomes more efficient, yielding more profits or more cash flow to reinvest into this data-centric approach.

While all theoretically correct, practically implementing the structural changes to realize this lifetime-value utopia requires not only a tech overhaul but, as discussed in Chapter 8, a company overhaul too.

UPSIDE FOR ALL

An increase in customer lifetime value is the ultimate upside for the enterprise. But as discussed in Chapter 2, data from product models also enable companies to build better products and, more importantly, products that will be bought. Feature prioritization and product line segmentation data are gold to product marketing. Companies can better connect with their prospects through more relevant marketing using highly targeted messaging that resonates with the customer needs observed in the data. It allows the brand to discover up-sell opportunities and new customer segments for entirely new products. It tethers support directly to the product, eliminating the guesswork for product repair and maintenance, reducing field dispatch costs, and increasing efficiency in spare parts inventory.

The customer also wins. The customer gets a better product with more useful functionality, making it more usable, efficient, and ultimately more reliable. And since maintenance is now proactive, predictive, or even prescriptive, the customer is more satisfied.

If this sounds like a business partnership, that's because it is. Anyone who's worked in business development or has been responsible for maintaining a fruitful business relationship between organizations knows this is hard. But it's easier with unfiltered data than without those data. Partnerships are key in IoT—both with customers and with other companies to deliver the outcomes your customers want. The interface between you and your customers and your partners is the data that the Internet of Things can deliver.

The new customer relationship is seductive because there's upside for all—the proverbial win-win situation. The point of sale is now just the beginning. The customer gets an evolving product that continuously meets its needs, and the enterprise is motivated to improve its business to increase customer lifetime value. This data-centric approach will forever transform the enterprise-customer relationship from shallow and casual to deep and long lasting.

• • •

Let's move on. Let's put the theory of Part One into action with Part Two by covering how to plan your IoT business and product line and then how to start executing it.

PART TWO

ANALYZING YOUR BUSINESS THROUGH THE IOT LENS

This is not a business plan book; there are as many of those resources as there are business planning philosophies. Instead, my approach is to develop an IoT lens through which you can look at any business and business plan. Heavy emphasis is placed on strategy, product requirements, and operations— the areas of the traditional business plan most affected by the Internet of Things. So consider this section as more of a plan on how to use IoT in your business than an IoT business plan template.

A majority of IoT products are developed without the support of a plan. That has to change to break out of the maker mindset. To me this is analogous to the tail wagging the dog, and it is the primary reason why I started the http://www.iot-inc.com media site and my http://www.brucesinclair.net consulting business. Without a step-by-step plan to guide our actions, we aren't working on a product; we're working on a hobby, and hobbies are for your spare time, not your business time. A business plan is needed to take tinkering to the next level.

This section is not theoretical. It comes directly from my consulting experience in helping brands develop their IoT business plans and product requirements. My clients have ranged from start-ups to multibillion-dollar conglomerates, but in all cases the initial engagement is the same: a two-day strategy session that yields a short, version 0.5, business plan. These sessions always start with education, beginning with the concepts covered in Parts One and Three of this book. I'm then educated about my clients' business: their customers, industry, competition, and current strategy. After day one is complete, we are ready for the second day, which systematically goes through a lot of the material covered in this section of the book. The information you will find in Part Two has been tested and honed in the real world from what I've learned from helping companies in consumer IoT, commercial IoT, industrial IoT, and infrastructure IoT. Let's get started!

CHAPTER 5

YOUR INDUSTRY AND THE CHANGES COMING

The current B2B sales narrative zeros in on solving customer problems: finding pain points and mitigating them. However, it's unusually rare that a single product or vendor can solve all the customer's problems. And if you think about it, the customer is not ultimately interested in solving point problems. The customer is interested in achieving outcomes, and products are simply a means to that end.

In a past life I worked for Softimage, a Microsoft subsidiary that developed and sold computer animation software for creating video games and movie special effects, including the dinosaurs that starred in all the *Jurassic Park* movies. The outcome our customer wanted was a realistic dinosaur, a dinosaur that looked so real, it would seamlessly blend into live-action movie footage. To get that level of realism, Industrial Light & Magic (ILM) needed to create a custom special effects pipeline that integrated products from multiple vendors. The wireframe object models of the dinosaurs that defined their shape were created by artists with one of our competitor's products. The dinosaurs were animated with our product. And they were rendered (colored) with an open-source renderer.

ILM then used a fourth product, this one a 2D compositor, from yet another company, to blend the 3D animation into the filmed 2D environment containing the actors and scenes. The animation pipeline, as it's called in the special effects industry, integrates point products and custom code to achieve a desired outcome. If you read the film credits after any special effects film, you will find these system integrators credited under the title of Technical Director (TD).

Sound familiar? Every industry has its own version of Technical Directors. Even when we consider discrete physical products, they too are "integrated" into some best-practice "pipeline." Reflecting back on our B2B value creation examples in Chapter 1, we recognize that the acetabular reamer is only one of the surgical tools used in the hip arthroplasty surgery pipeline. The electric grid is in the center of the electricity pipeline, connecting power production to power consumption. The bucket wheel excavator is at the beginning of the pipeline of mining assets, all orchestrated to produce and deliver coal to the power plant.

Business today creates ad hoc pipelines, integrating point products from different vendors together in order to deliver the outcome they desire. Let's start there; let's start with outcomes.

YOUR CUSTOMERS AND THEIR DESIRED OUTCOMES

Your strategic analysis begins by clearly understanding the desired outcome of your customers. All customers have a desired outcome—what they actually want—and rarely, except for the simplest of cases, can it be delivered by a single product. Like ILM's quest to create realistic dinosaurs for *Jurassic Park*, customers often act as their own system integrator, stitching together all the products they need to achieve their desired outcome. Same thing for business models. Customers stitch together the business models of multiple products and associate them with the revenue they generate in order to define an ROI and, they hope, a profitable P&L.

By virtualizing the physical product into a software-defined product, we can use application programming interfaces (APIs) for the stitching-together part to bring together multiple products and their business models. This is how it is done in the software world, and it is still how ILM does it today: by interfacing software together. In IoT this will not happen overnight; however, over time, more physical products will use their software twins to interface with each other and be orchestrated to help provide more of what the customers really want. Customers don't want point products; they want specific outcomes. IoT tech can help make that happen, and if it can happen, it will happen because it's something customers will pay for. And if it will happen, this should be incorporated into your strategic planning and influence your daily decisions. It won't happen in the short term, but including this future into your current thinking will provide your company with a strategic advantage over its competitors. And your competitors may not be who you think . . .

Examples

Let's go through our four value creation product examples introduced in Chapter 2. When first discussed, we considered their value propositions. Now we are looking at the outcome they are part of achieving to reinforce the concept of desired outcomes (see Figure 5.1).

No matter how impressive the acetabular reamer is, no hospital really wants to own one. Just like their other surgical instruments, it's a tool to be used with other tools. In this case the outcome the hospital wants is to *replace the hip as quickly and as safely as possible.*

| Figure 5.1 | **Desired outcome examples** |

To be healthier and look better

Replace hip as quickly and as safely as possible

CONSUMER

COMMERCIAL

INFRASTRUCTURE

Extract and deliver coal

Have reliable and efficient energy delivery

INDUSTRIAL

The utility company has no interest in financing and owning infrastructure. The electric grid is plumbing, moving electricity from the power plant to its end users. As a business, the utility company wants more reliability and less waste. Put another way, the outcome it wants is *reliable and efficient energy delivery*.

Although bigger . . . much bigger . . . the bucket wheel excavator is also just a tool, in this case, to scrape coal out of the ground. But what the mining company wants—the outcome it wants—is to *extract and deliver coal*. The last thing it wants is to own a $100 million machine sitting on the balance sheet depreciating while incurring large interest and operational expenses.

If consumers really wanted quantified self wearables, 75 percent of them would not be stashed away in a drawer nine months after being bought. Although fun gadgets to play with, the outcome consumers really want is to *be healthier and look better*.

So if we were to deliver the outcomes that the customers of these four products really want, we would be selling fast and safe surgeries, effective extraction, dependable and efficient electricity delivery, and better health and looks.

Consider your customers and ask yourself, what outcome do they really want? Then, where does your product or product line fit into that overall result? What does their pipeline look like?

Next we will see how focusing on outcomes, instead of products, will rewire industries.

Unexpected Consequences

Let me use an example from my client, ACME Pest, that I discussed a couple of times earlier in the book. When you think pest control, the first thing that comes to mind is the mousetrap. And that's exactly what ACME sells, mousetraps. It sells them through a two-layer channel—through large distributors, which then sell them to pest control companies, which in the commercial world sell them as part of their services to hospitals, high-rise buildings, and food processing plants. Hospitals, high-rise buildings, and food processing plants may use mousetraps, but they don't want them, and they certainly don't want to deal with anything caught inside! What they really want is a pest-free environment. That is the outcome the customer wants. A mousetrap is a means to that end, but as it turns out, not the only one.

Pest management is broader than most people think. There are actually three parts to delivering a pest-free environment: cleanliness, integrity, and what I'll call security, that is, catching the mice. If your environment is clean, mice aren't interested. If the integrity of your environment is sound, that is, if the building's perimeter is solid, mice can't get in. The mousetrap comes into play if and only if the mouse makes it through the perimeter because it smelled something appetizing in the unclean environment. So again, the desired outcome is not to catch (and then dispose of) a mouse; it is to have no mice at all.

Delivering desired outcomes should be thought of on two dimensions: value creation and monetization. Value creation will provide as much of the outcome as possible, and monetization will provide a business model that is as close as possible to the customer's business model. To deliver your customer's desired outcome means your company must work with other companies—companies that may end up being partners, competitors, or consolidators.

THE IOT TECH CONTINUUM

Consider the evolution of products (see Figure 5.2). Starting out as "dumb" products, they evolve to include a form of local intelligence (embedded chipset) to make them smart. Smart products are then tethered to a mobile device for command and control, making them connected products. Beyond connected products, we are now witnessing the emergence of the IoT product. This is where things get interesting, and more importantly, this is where value starts popping.

Figure 5.2	**Product evolution**

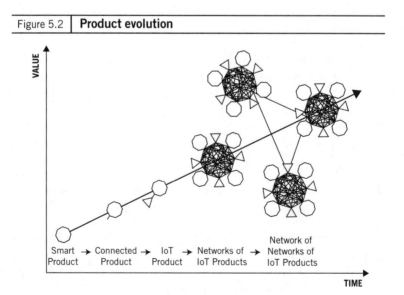

When IoT products connect to each other, we have a network of IoT products, working together, generally as a product line from a single vendor. And finally, products evolve into networks of these networks of IoT products—product lines from different vendors, working together to deliver the customer's desired outcome. They are brought together technically with IoT platforms and monetized as ecosystems.

More Than Just Better Mousetraps

Let's see how this plays out in pest management that includes sanitation, construction, and extermination. Within each of these industries, enterprises will first build their smart products with some local intelligence. They will then build connected products that offer remote control functionality as well as perhaps remote viewing. Not that exciting yet. After realizing connected products don't provide enough value to justify their price, they will create IoT products that connect to external systems. IoT platforms will emerge in each industry as companies build out their portfolios of IoT products networked into IoT product lines.

OK, let's pause here to see what we have.

In the sanitation market, smart products will lead to connected floor and drain cleaners, which will evolve to include sensor arrays to measure and analyze bacteria and other pathogens. Then a sanitation IoT product portfolio that includes cleaning systems, disposal systems, and chemical management products will emerge.

Similarly, in construction, smart tools will lead to connected tools, which will lead to IoT tools that find structural problems (like openings) in floors, walls, and ceilings through the use of sensing and analytics technology. As the construction industry expands its product offerings to include smart building technology, it will also be able to tap into services that can notify building owners when doors and windows are left open, to prevent walking, crawling, and flying pests from entering the environment.

In extermination, smart traps will lead to connected traps with notification and remote viewing, which will lead to IoT mouse-traps that will talk to each other and use analytics to improve their effectiveness. A portfolio of rodent, insect, and flying insect IoT trap products will emerge.

All right, lots of innovation, but the best part comes next. We then have IoT product lines for sanitation, construction, and extermination, each consisting of highly integrated point products.

The next step is a big one. It's the convergence of each of these separate product lines into a suite of product lines. This ecosystem is technically supported by a common IoT platform. But it is the monetization of these different product lines by an ecosystem that fuels the customer's outcome.

Partnerships, Partnerships, Partnerships

The IoT Tech Continuum will bring together sanitation, construction, extermination, and other new types of partnerships to deliver what customers really want. This is all related to partnerships: establishing them, technically supporting them, and making money from them.

For ACME Pest, it is a competitive advantage to know, before its competitors do, that their industry is going in the direction of close collaboration with sanitation and building maintenance. Having the foresight to work with companies within sanitation and building maintenance, before any other company, is a competitive advantage. It doesn't mean the extermination products need to start talking to the products from the other two industries on day one; instead it means that business partnerships should be initiated as a first step. Perhaps it's simply a joint marketing relationship or a distribution agreement or even a sales relationship that brings the two business models a little closer together. Partnerships also imply that a common IoT platform should be used for their future products and that one or more companies in these three industries are going to emerge to establish that platform and accompanying ecosystem. The biggest spoils will go to the ecosystem company, and that company generally will be the one that acts first.

MORE EXAMPLES

Let's look again at our four product examples to speculate on their evolution from individual IoT products, to product lines of IoT products, and then to platforms of product lines to deliver an outcome (see Figure 5.3).

Commercial IoT

Desired outcome: Replace the hip as quickly and as safely as possible.

Product: IoT acetabular reamer.

Figure 5.3	Platform/ecosystem examples

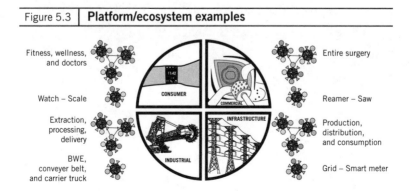

Product line: The two main orthopedic activities during hip replacement surgery are drilling and sawing, so it would make sense to network the acetabular reamer and the oscillating surgical saw into a product line to coordinate their activities.

Platform: Expanded out further, all instruments and machines used during the surgery—and the operating room itself—would be connected by an IoT platform.

Infrastructure IoT

Desired outcome: Have reliable and efficient energy delivery.

Product: IoT grid.

Product line: Buying just the right amount of electricity from power wholesalers has a big impact on the utility's profitability, so accurately estimating the power consumption in advance of need is paramount. In the past, home meters would be read by utility personnel, say once a month. Their data would be consolidated by hand to yield a month-by-month history, on a block-by-block basis, in order to estimate need. In contrast, smart meters provide an hour-by-hour history, on a home-by-home basis, yielding far more data to make more accurate purchase decisions. A grid connects power sources to power destinations (sinks), so a natural product line would be the grid and smart meter.

Platform: A power platform will bring together power plants, grid, microgrids, and smart meters, to help utilities to make buy, sell and utilization decisions based on consumption, pricing, and environmental data.

Industrial IoT

Desired outcome: Extract and deliver coal.

Product: IoT BWE.

Product line: Strip mining, the form of coal mining performed by the bucket wheel excavator, involves extracting a coal vein and then, depending on its quality, either transporting the coal and its accompanying overburden to a processing plant to remove impurities or preparing it for transport. A logical product line is the IoT BWE, conveyer belt, and carrier truck.

Platform: A mining platform would also include processing machinery and the complete transportation chain, which would consist of not only conveyer belts and carrier trucks onsite, but also long-haul trucks, rail, and water shipping to transport the coal to the power plant to be burned to produce electricity.

Consumer IoT

Desired outcome: Be healthier and look better

Product: IoT watch.

Product line: If the watch, with its virtual trainer, were sold with a bathroom scale, analytics could correlate activity with weight changes and modify the training program.

Platform: Guided by the bigger goal of better health, the platform would connect the product line to a food consumption app, a gym's exercise equipment, medical records, a grocery store's inventory . . . and the list goes on.

REWIRING INDUSTRIES

The changes in IoT tech and business models that will rewire your industry will have implications that must be taken into account when developing your IoT strategy.

Shifting Boundaries of Competition

As we saw in the pest management example, competition will change. Today an extermination company does not consider a national sanitation conglomerate as competition; but it could be. In fact, you could make the case that sanitation, extermination, and construction are equally qualified to extend their business into integrated pest management by providing the platform (tech) and ecosystem (business) to attract companies from the other two industries to join them in providing their joint customer with the outcome they want.

Shifting to consumer IoT, the smart home market also provides some nonintuitive examples to reflect on. Would you expect Google with the Nest thermostat and security company ADT to be competitors? Well, they are, and so is practically every other company that has a smart home product, from Philips (lights) to Amazon Echo (speaker) to Petzila (remote pet feeders). The big play in the smart home vertical is the same big play in every industry vertical: to control the ecosystem.

Every company that provides part of the outcome the customer wants can build out from its solution with an IoT platform to attract the missing parts of the overall outcome and, in the process, control the ecosystem—which manages the business model, distribution, and ultimately the customer.

Typically, when crossing the chasm curve, we see start-ups addressing the needs of early adopters, and it is only after the market has matured that you typically see large, established companies entering the fray. But not in the Outcome Economy. The desire to establish *the* ecosystem explains why there is so much interest today in the smart home by so many big players—Amazon, Google, Philips, ADT, Apple, Samsung, Walmart, GE . . . for what is, today, a very small market. All these companies are not there for today's revenue; they're in it to stake their claim for the long game, trying to establish or be a dominant player in one of the ecosystems that will emerge in the smart home space. It's all about competing at the ecosystem layer, here and in every other industry vertical.

Disintermediating the Vulnerable

The new, intimate customer relationship that comes with IoT brings with it new business opportunities. Multitier distribution is at risk if the distribution channel is solely an intermediary extracting its pound of flesh. Tesla has disintermediated the car dealer. Tesla sells directly to the customer, and the relationship starts from there. Remember that "new car smell" enabled by Tesla's OTA feature update mechanism? There's no need for a dealer (intermediary) in that scenario. No need to work through an indirect layer of distribution to access the customer. Tesla and their customers have a direct relationship. And it doesn't stop at distribution.

What if Tesla sold car insurance to its customers; would you buy it? Would you buy it if it were 40 percent cheaper than any other insurance? By having that 24-hour-a-day, 7-day-a-week view into its drivers' habits, Tesla could selectively offer lower-cost but still highly profitable insurance to those drivers who, according to predictive analytics, have a much lower probability of getting into trouble in the future. Having this direct and intimate customer relationship expands business in unpredictable ways, potentially disintermediating those companies with less meaningful relationships.

When looking at your industry through the IoT lens, can your company cut out any layers of distribution? Can your company leverage its intimate customer relationship to better sell auxiliary products typically sold by another company? This disintermediation, of course cuts both ways. Is there a company out there, not on your competitive radar, that could cut you out or sell you out if it had the intimate relationship instead of you?

Subsuming Conventional Product Categories

I've been an age-group amateur triathlete for 15 years. When I first got into the sport, I was obsessed with quantifying my activities and using the analytics website that came with my Garmin sports watch, to correlate my heart rate with running pace and my cycling power with speed. Before my first Ironman I hired a coach that pored over my analytics to determine when I was fatigued or when I could be pushed just a little bit harder. The problem was that the sports watch was big and bulky and you had to wear an uncomfortable and expensive heart rate strap around your chest. This category of product, the sports watch, is being subsumed by the quantified self, or smart watch. Sleeker, easier to use, and more high tech, these watches are superior products built for the larger, more casual market but also attractive to the sports market. The next time I upgrade, I'll choose a smart watch that includes sports functionality with a lower price, requires no chest strap, and includes better analytics, eliminating the need for a coach. IoT tech can make what used to be specialized, commoditized. Can any of your products become the subset of a bigger product or a component of another product line?

Changing Business Models

Industries can also be rewired by innovative business models that allow customers to pay in a way that more closely matches the business models and therefore their preferences. Internet of Things technology allows us to measure, among other things, KPIs from our customers' business models. Business models were extensively discussed in Chapter 3.

The service business model enables the sharing economy, but up to this time, the sharing economy has been based on big-ticket items such as cars and homes. This is partially because of the underlying IT infrastructure needed to commercially implement the product-as-a-service (PaaS) business model. With IoT, most of this infrastructure is already built in, so practically any physical product can support this service business model. What's important is not to try to necessarily mimic the business models of Zipcar or Airbnb but to recognize that your business model is going to become an increasingly important feature—one that can dramatically change your industry. Consider the disruption currently happening in the automotive industry caused by IoT cars (autonomous vehicles) and the IoT-enabling business model that will be applied to them. If this is what's possible with the service business model, imagine the transformational potential of the outcome business model.

IoT is information technology and as such will support the "business model as a feature." The power of SaaS, which has redefined the software industry, can now be applied to physical products. Outside of the software industry, that's shifting away from software licenses, another good example is fintech (financial technology), as exemplified by the application CashMe. As used by my family, it allows my wife and me to easily and instantly add cash to our teenagers' bank accounts. I also use it to get paid for part of my business. This application disintermediates banks and credit card companies through peer-to-peer banking, gaining market share by a business model that does not include charging a transaction fee.

ACCELERATED INDUSTRY MATURATION

The dynamics associated with a rewiring will accelerate industry maturation, forcing incumbents to strategically address the forces of consolidation and commoditization on their business earlier than anticipated.

Consolidation

Over time, consolidation in your industry will happen at the product and then ecosystem levels; the question is, how soon? At the product level, the first mover's advantage and barriers to entry (discussed in Chapter 6) afforded to early IoT companies will limit the number of IoT products within each category. And the overwhelming competitive advantages of an IoT product over a traditional product are such that the new IoT product will prune the number of traditional products in its segment, if not eliminate them completely.

Let's say there are two acetabular reamers for sale. One is the traditional reamer, the same design used for decades, and the second reamer, the IoT reamer, is guaranteed not to burn out and kill bone cells, giving the hip implant a much higher chance of success. Plus, the IoT reamer will provide data that can be analyzed to make hip replacement surgeries more successful in other ways. And furthermore, the IoT acetabular reamer will be sold with a more hospital-friendly business model. Of the two products, which one do you think the hospital will buy?

As we are seeing today in these early days of ecosystems, every IoT company has dreams of establishing its industry's ecosystem. But this can't last. Darwinian market forces will prevail, leaving each industry supported by only a few ecosystems. The implications are twofold. If your company wants to establish an ecosystem, know you're in it for the long haul and you will have competition commensurate with the market's size. This will require a major investment. And second, even if your company does not establish an ecosystem, you still need to be part of one. Like ecosystems at the macro level, each ecosystem will only support a few companies for each product category. There will be scarcity at both levels, so plan for this now, even if it's only part of your company's long-term strategy.

Commoditization

Similar to consolidation but on a different timeline, products that fail to adapt to become IoT products within a formal or informal ecosystem will be commoditized. Just as is done today, integrating these lone wolf stand-alone products into a full solution will require hard coding by a system integrator or design house, assembling a custom ecosystem for the customer. In doing so, the assembler owns the customer relationship and has control over the stand-alone product manufacturer, delegating them to the role of a less valued OEM supplier. By definition, this loss of control and competitiveness leads to commoditization.

• • •

Industry implications to consider for your IoT strategy are wide and deep but can't be considered in isolation. The next key component of your IoT strategy is your competition, considered in the next chapter.

CHAPTER 6

IOT COMPETITION AND IOT COMPETITIVE ADVANTAGES

For me, assessing competition in the Internet of Things brings to mind the infamous quote by Donald Rumsfeld, former U.S. Secretary of Defense. During a Department of Defense news briefing in 2002, he stated, "Reports that say that something hasn't happened are always interesting to me, because as we know, there are known knowns; there are things we know we know. We also know there are known unknowns; that is to say we know there are some things we do not know. But there are also unknown unknowns—the ones we don't know we don't know."

Even though he wasn't the first to apply the Johari window to intelligence matters and the quote was criticized by some to be an opaque deflection of a hard question, I like it. And sure, like a haiku, you can read into it what you want, but I like it because it nicely frames the competitive landscape for any company considering the launch of an IoT product.

These are largely the three classes of competitors that companies entering the market with an Internet of Things product will face: existing competitors, left-field competitors, and new entrants. This chapter examines these three classes of competition and the unique reasons why market entry timing is critical to each. Then the common competitive advantages of entering a market early are viewed from the IoT lens.

EXISTING COMPETITORS—THE KNOWN KNOWNS

You know who the known knowns are because you're already competing with them. And if they survive, they will continue to compete against you using IoT. First it will be IoT product versus traditional product, and then IoT product versus IoT product, and finally IoT product versus IoT product in the ecosystem.

> **TECH TALK**
>
> Examine the ecosystem— all competitors will be part of an ecosystem. See Chapter 7.

They are the competitors most like you today, meaning they have no inherent IoT competitive advantages to begin with. Assuming an equal playing field, the advantages to gain over these competitors are related to timing. Which competitor is likely to launch an IoT product first, and should your company preempt this anticipated first strike or follow? And then, which competitor is likely to create or join an ecosystem first? As discussed in the last chapter, there are only going to be so many ecosystem slots available per industry, so the concept of scarcity can also be used to your advantage if you move early.

LEFT-FIELD COMPETITORS— THE KNOWN UNKNOWNS

The known unknowns are future ecosystem competitors. If your company is planning to establish an ecosystem or thinking about establishing an ecosystem, then you need to consider this class of competitors. Not because they will compete with your product but because they will compete against your ecosystem. Although seemingly coming out of left field, if you reverse-engineer your customer's desired outcome, you can identify this category of competitors. If your company plans on establishing an ecosystem, then it will compete with the other companies that contribute to the customer's outcome that also want to establish an ecosystem.

Companies from other industries that you never considered competitive before are the known unknowns. For example, who would expect a thermostat to be competitive with a door lock, to be competitive with lights, to be competitive with security? We would. They're competitors because each of the companies that produce these products wants to establish and own the home IoT ecosystem. The timing of when to apply the resources to launch and grow an ecosystem is a strategic decision.

NEW ENTRANTS—THE UNKNOWN UNKNOWNS

The unknown unknowns are, by definition, the most difficult competitors to anticipate. The competitors in this category won't necessarily have domain experience, but they will have software and data science backgrounds along with a great idea for a product that competes with yours. An example of this is playing out in fintech. High-tech start-ups with little financial experience or history are taking on status quo traditional banks, insurance companies, and investment institutions. These types of competitors aren't limited to start-ups; they

TECH TALK

Competing outside and inside the ecosystem. For more information on ecosystems see Chapter 7.

can be large too—for example, Google now makes physical devices for the home.

Consider that an IoT product exists in two forms: the techy software-defined product and the traditional physical product. The question is, for any particular customer and market, which of the two forms provides the greatest competitive advantage?

The traditional incumbent has many advantages. It has a brand, knows the market, has distribution, and, most importantly, has customers. It relies on the excellence of its physical design and feature set and how well the traditional product is manufactured. The traditional incumbent's disadvantage is having less technical capability, specifically in the disciplines of software development and data science, both critical to building an IoT product.

The unknown unknown competitor is free of legacy products baggage and politics and brings with it a rich history from the Internet world and core competencies in building applications, creating models, and building analytic frameworks for analysis. The unknown unknown competitor knows tech but is new to the industry vertical.

Which company is more competitive? The incumbent, playing defense, with an existing business that is strong in manufacturing but relatively weak in software and data science, or the unknown unknown new entrant, playing offense, with experience in building software-defined products but with relatively less manufacturing experience and virtually no industry presence? (See Table 6.1.)

Depending on the magnitude of the incremental value created by the new entrant's IoT product, the answer will be different and will change over time. Over time, the new entrant will learn the industry and become more established. Over time, the incumbent will develop IoT functionality. Whether your company is the incumbent or new entrant, estimate when these two curves are likely to cross, and from there, work backward to determine your go-to-market timing (see Figure 6.1).

Table 6.1	Competitive Advantages

New Entrants	Incumbents
Software know-how	Brand awareness
Data science know-how	Distribution
Internet know-how	Customers
Free of legacy baggage	Physical design
	Manufacturing

Figure 6.1	Relative competitive advantages

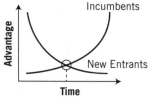

Relative Product Advantage

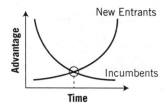

Relative Business Advantage

THE ADVANTAGES OF EMPLOYING IOT EARLY

The Internet of Things is not a question of *if*, it's a question of *when*: when should my company begin with IoT? The answer is now, at least for the planning phase that's covered in this book. The more expensive question is, when should my company commit human resources and budget to go from our business plan and requirements to our proof-of-concept, prototype, and then minimum viable product? As we just discussed, deciding when to enter the market with an IoT offering is critical for competing with all three classes of competitors—each with its own unique reasons. Launch too early and you or your customers may not be ready. Launch too late and your company may be at a disadvantage to a first mover, or face insurmountable barriers to entry, or have to compete with an IoT company that has developed other unfair competitive advantages over you. Let's look at these challenges, one by one.

First-Mover Advantages

There are many advantages associated with entering the market first with an IoT product.

IoT years are like dog years, at least when it comes to product development. The IoT product manager has a gusher of customer data coming in daily. Interpreted by analytics, this is a new and major source of input for product improvement. If the company's engineering organization has been oriented to act upon this information with agile procedures, then each year of data-driven product refinement is like seven years of refinements in the non-IoT product world. Here's the thinking behind my estimate.

When working in the physical product domain, development cycles are long—12 months at least to deliver a new version. In my first career as a software developer, we had major releases every six to nine months, and if we were lucky, we had minor releases every quarter. Now, if implemented properly, IoT software can be combined with automatic OTA updates to eliminate discrete releases entirely. Just as with cloud computing, software changes to the IoT product can now occur daily if not more frequently. The IoT company can iterate on its products quicker, which, in turn, quickly builds differentiating value. And not only will the IoT product evolve at a much quicker rate, but so too will the business model and organizational structure, making the IoT company more competitive by moving first.

The second competitive advantage to consider is the changed customer relationship. As discussed in Chapter 4, this close, win-

win relationship forges a strong bond. Trying to "unstick" key accounts will be difficult after they have developed into close relationships. Being late to this party can be an existential threat.

Longer term, companies will compete within or as part of an ecosystem. In the Outcome Economy there will be three types of IoT companies. Lone wolves that only offer stand-alone IoT products, pack wolves whose IoT products are part of an ecosystem, and alpha wolves, companies that commercialize their own ecosystem and invite others to join.

Every competitive IoT company either will be in an ecosystem or will found an ecosystem. Since each industry will only be able to support a limited number of ecosystems, and since within each of these ecosystems there will be a place for only a limited number of players within each product category, space is . . . well, limited, making moving first, or at least early, strategic.

Early entrants will have a competitive advantage over their lagging competitors by filling those limited ecosystem spots. Developing an ecosystem will be even more competitive. It's a major undertaking requiring considerable resources, but alpha wolves will enjoy a sustainable unfair advantage over their competitors, making timing for this type of company even more competitive.

Barriers to Entry

Related to first-mover advantages are the competitive barriers to entry established by first movers. Although pure software patents have weakened in recent years, method patents are flourishing. What is a method patent if not a recipe for bringing together the different systems within an IoT product? These are still early days, but this type of intellectual property is ripe to be grown, picked, and stored in company patent portfolios for future offensive and defensive purposes. Patents, especially in an emerging space like IoT, represent a formidable barrier to entry for latecomers, big and small. Not publicly protecting your IoT trade secrets early can lead to future problems.

Related is the scarcity in talent to develop this intellectual property. The talent pool is small enough, but talent with domain experience is in even shorter supply. This talent pool will only go down during the early years of IoT. Finding and keeping this talent creates a tall barrier to entry.

Other Competitive Advantages

One of the most profound operational implications, which will be discussed later in Chapter 8, is the change required in a company's human resource DNA. Every company will have talent gaps, especially in the areas of software development and data science. While software developers with the skills needed for server, client, embedded, and cloud development are not easy to find and compete for, they exist. More difficult to find will be the data scientists required to put the analytics systems into place to transform the volumes of data into useful information. The later the company enters the IoT market, the scarcer both these types of talent will be, especially talent that also has domain experience. DNA changes are not limited to engineering. Changes also must occur in every other department. Mutating early is a notable advantage.

Lastly, we come down to supply and demand. Early Internet of Things products will outcompete their traditional, less valuable counterparts. In doing so they build market share. Like the traditional products before them, each market will only support so many IoT products per category, especially when they are part of an ecosystem.

. . .

These competitive advantages are formidable. Timing is everything. The ramifications of being late or early need to be part of every enterprise's calculus when timing its market entry.

In the next chapter we discuss the big picture: the Outcome Economy. IoT makes your company more competitive today, but in the future, it will be the prerequisite for competition.

CHAPTER 7

THE OUTCOME ECONOMY

Eric Soderlund had the cool and confident demeanor you'd expect from a general, and in some ways, I guess he was like a general, a general tasked with guarding a cookie fortress.

Eric was prospect number eight of nine in our first-round product validation trip, where ACME Pest and I were out selling our newly conceived IoT mousetrap, and in the process, gaining valuable insights into how to make the product better. This visit was a little different though. Instead of us going to the customer, Eric came up from North Carolina because we wanted to *design-sell-build* (the validation process I use, explained in Chapter 10) with a large food processing customer, representing one of ACME Pest's largest market segments. So instead of meeting at his factory, Eric flew in for a quick one-day, one-night, all-expenses-paid trip to New York City to meet us in a borrowed boardroom in the center of the Financial District, only a couple of blocks from our meeting earlier in the day at Confident Surroundings Pest Management.

Unlike prospects Paul Brass and Pat Dronski, who worked for pest control companies, Eric oversaw quality assurance for the biggest factory of one of the largest cookie manufacturers in the country. He ran his pest management mission, among others, with military precision. Eric had only one fear, but it was a big one, one that could pop out of nowhere at any time: the audit. If, at any time, health inspectors found *any* evidence of a mouse, they could shut down the entire plant. Immediately. Jobs were on the line, and so too was the company's bottom line. The mission was clear: keep the enemy (mice) out at any cost. Although he had built up his perimeter defenses and even augmented them with infrared cameras, he needed more.

Parts of any audit, especially the BRC audit, were subjective. There were no mice in *his house*, so if things did go wrong, Eric needed deniability and an audit trail with data to back him up. He saw our product, with its reams of stored mouse activity data, as being able to do that.

The outcome Eric wanted was a clean and healthy environment that passed audit.

BILLIONS AND TRILLIONS

One of the things IoT is best known for is its hype. Analysts and vendors alike are locked in an arms race to conceive of the biggest and most wide-reaching predictions for the size of the IoT market and for its impact on business. These are all big numbers: billions of things and trillions of dollars.

They are economy-size numbers. In fact, as we'll see at the end of this chapter, these types of numbers can only be generated by the Outcome Economy, and IoT is the technical enabler of the commerce that will make those numbers real.

Our economy is changing. It's currently composed of the supply and demand of products, but the popularity of buying and selling services (XaaS, or anything as a service, not to be confused with the service industry) is on the rise, and it doesn't end there. On the horizon is the Outcome Economy. Based on the supply and demand of outcomes, the Outcome Economy is one completely infused with IoT technology. No longer will there be tech and nontech industries. Like the Internet today, the Internet of Things will become part of all industries, receding into the background, being everywhere but nowhere at the same time.

Whoa, that's pretty far out there, right? Yeah, this is not going to happen overnight, but knowing how the long game is going to play out will help you plan your short game. Since I'm Canadian, I'll use the cliché from hockey great Wayne Gretzky, who said, "Skate to where the puck is going to be, not where it has been."

THE UNDERPINNING OF
THE OUTCOME ECONOMY

Eric Soderlund doesn't want to own any mousetraps, and he especially doesn't want the mice inside; he just wants the mousetrap to do its magic for his cookie factory: to keep it a clean and healthy environment that passes inspection.

To provide this outcome, three industries must be involved. You need sanitation to keep the environment clean, to not attract mice. You need construction to maintain the building's integrity, to block the mice from entering. And only after the mice have smelled something good and have somehow found their way inside, do you want to catch them.

Therefore, to provide what Eric really wants, we must bring together the technology and the business of sanitation, construction, and extermination. Luckily there are two trends that are making this possible. I've described them earlier as the IoT Tech

Continuum (Chapter 5) and the IoT Business Model Continuum (Chapter 3), both of which are enabled by the Internet of Things.

The IoT Platform

The IoT platform brings it all together technically (see Figure 7.1). It orchestrates the products necessary to achieve the customer's outcome.

The IoT platform plays a key role in the IoT Tech Continuum, bringing together the four components of the IoT product (software-defined product, hardware-defined product, external systems, and network fabric), bringing together the IoT products from a vendor to create product lines, and finally bringing together IoT product lines from different vendors to support the IoT ecosystem.

In this example, the same technical evolution is happening in parallel in the sanitation, construction, and extermination indus-

| Figure 7.1 | **Bring products together** |

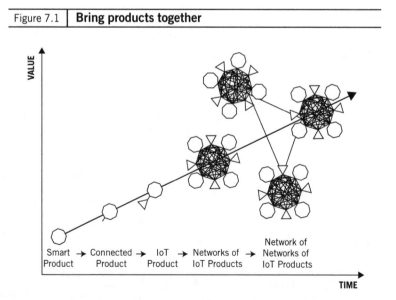

tries. At the end of the continuum we have a network of these three IoT products lines, all working together on a common IoT platform.

This is the technical underpinning of the ecosystem and the Outcome Economy.

The IoT Business Model

The IoT business model describes how a company monetizes the IoT value it creates.

As the business model evolves from product to service to outcome (see Figure 7.2), IoT enables us to measure both the key performance variables in the cookie maker's business model and the relative contributions of sanitation, construction, and extermination to that outcome, structuring the ecosystem's business model.

This is the commercial underpinning of the ecosystem (see Figure 7.3) and the Outcome Economy. IoT enables the platform and business model necessary to create an ecosystem to deliver a specific outcome.

| Figure 7.2 | **The IoT Business Model Continuum** |

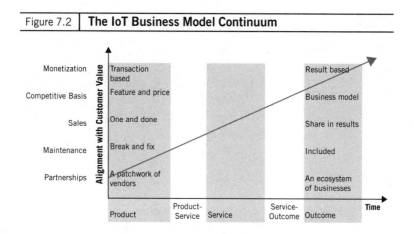

Figure 7.3 | IoT Technology to enable the ecosystem

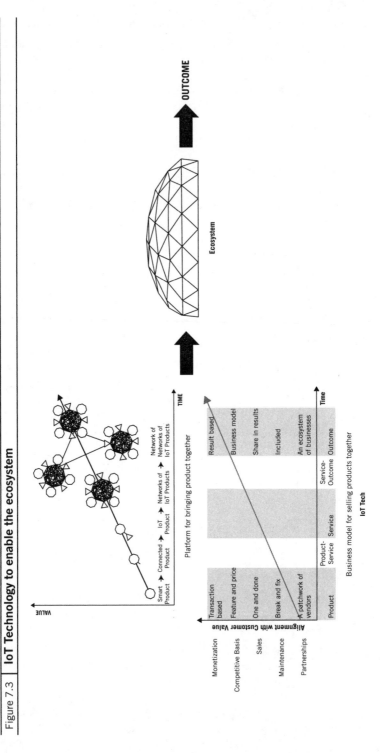

THE ECOSYSTEM—THE BUILDING BLOCK OF THE OUTCOME ECONOMY

The purpose of an ecosystem is to deliver a specific outcome. It is an outcome machine that brings together the producers (vendors) and the consumers (customers) of the IoT tech in order to monetize it.

Value chains are linear, but ecosystems are nonlinear, are more interconnected, and can be better described as a value mesh, which neatly follows Metcalfe's law of value. Hence, it's good to be an ecosystem provider that manages the primary relationship with the customer and the overall ecosystem business model.

Each ecosystem will have multiple vendors and multiple customers. In our case, ACME and vendors from sanitation and construction work together with Eric's commercial bakery to deliver a clean and healthy environment that passes inspection (see Figure 7.4).

Figure 7.4	Pest management ecosystem

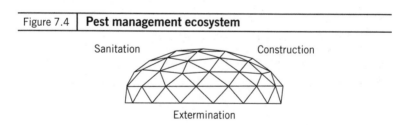

Sanitation   Construction

Extermination

Information

IoT ecosystems are still gathering critical mass. Unlike in the smartphone industry whose ecosystems have coalesced around operating systems like iOS (platform) with the App Store (ecosystem) and Android (platform) with Google Play (ecosystem), IoT is broader. While predicting its ecosystems will form in the same way may seem logical, current evidence suggests otherwise. Unlike in the smartphone industry that only has a few ecosystems applicable to all markets, ecosystems in IoT will be more numerous and form differently based on the market segment. They will also form differently. The current state of the art indicates that ecosystems are primarily coalescing around devices in consumer IoT, around stand-alone IoT platforms (commercial, in-house, and open source) in commercial IoT, around consortia in industrial IoT, and around dominant vendors in infrastructure IoT. This, however, will likely change with maturation.

The lack of standards is certainly slowing progress. While all the expected standard bodies and consortia, and even government bodies, are doing their best to ratify something all stakeholders can agree on, we may end up seeing de facto standards win at the end of the day—decided by customer dollars spent rather than industry votes cast. Parts of the platform will standardize across all industries, but the ends, working toward the middle, won't; the ends—being the sensors and analytics—will continue to be domain specific.

But don't let the lack of standardization slow you. As recommended earlier in the book, start partnering with the organizations whose products can be offered with yours to form a heterogeneous product line. This is the beginning of an ecosystem, and this will start your company on the path of delivering outcomes to your customers.

Ecosystem Evolution

Companies will take part in different ecosystems, each to satisfy a different outcome for its business. Similarly, vendors will also join one or more ecosystems. Over time ecosystems will merge or grow to deliver higher-level, bigger outcomes, encompassing more and more outcomes within their industry (see Figure 7.5).

Figure 7.5	Ever-increasing ecosystem

   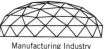

Clean and Healthy   Quality Assurance   Production   Manufacturing Industry

Eric's bigger outcome goes beyond clean and healthy. His department is responsible for the cookie plant's overall quality assurance (QA), which also includes raw material preparation, equipment calibration, and packaging. A natural evolution of a clean and healthy ecosystem into a QA ecosystem would include instrumenting food safety, food quality, and food testing. You can predict where this goes. The QA ecosystem then expands into a production ecosystem (baking cookies), and finally, when the commercial baker's entire business is considered, this production ecosystem would be bookended by a supply chain ecosystem up front and a distribution ecosystem on the back end, merging into the larger manufacturing ecosystem that would encompass all three—the entire value mesh of food manufacturing.

As in food manufacturing, each industry's ecosystems will grow to solve more and more of the customer's problem until there are only a few ecosystems per industry.

It is this coming together of different ecosystems that realizes the Outcome Economy.

THE NEW NEW ECONOMY

An Outcome Economy is the sum of all ecosystem business activity within a geographic location (see Figure 7.6).

An example Outcome Economy consisting of some of the main examples used in this book includes:

- The buying and selling of outcomes in the mining industry

- The buying and selling of surgical outcomes (such as the hip replacement), which, when combined with quantified self outcomes, could be broadened to the buying and selling of health and wellness outcomes for joint replacements

- The buying and selling of energy outcomes—starting in the coal mine and ending at a hospital

Using this example for any geographic region, this Outcome Economy would be the sum of a mining ecosystem, a health and wellness ecosystem, and an energy ecosystem (see Figure 7.7).

Figure 7.6	Various ecosystems will emerge for each of these industries

		BUSINESS	
CONSUMER IoT	**COMMERCIAL IoT**	**INDUSTRIAL IoT**	**INFRASTRUCTURE IoT**
• Wearables	• Transportation	• Manufacturing	• Smart grid
• Consumer goods	• Healthcare	• Mining	• Utilities
• Smart homes	• Smart buildings	• Oil and Gas	• Smart cities
	• Defense and gov.	• Agriculture	
	• Insurance		
	• Finance		

The Network Effect Yielding Billions and Trillions

Economic shifts are primarily driven by new value creation. The emergence of the Service Economy can be credited to new value creation, but this value in the Service Economy (XaaS—anything as a service) is primarily derived by new methods of consumption rather than fundamental changes to the product (X). The Outcome Economy (see Figure 7.8), that is, the supply and demand of outcomes, is different—and bigger. The Outcome Economy is being driven by incremental value creation and incremental value consumption, both enabled by the Internet of Things.

Figure 7.7	**Ecosystems in a region**

Figure 7.8	**Outcome economy**

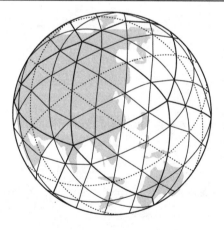

Remember, all incremental value created by an IoT product comes from transforming its data into useful information. The more data, the more (accurate) information and the more value. This is core to explaining the mega numbers being attributed to the Internet of Things.

By definition, the Internet of Things benefits from the network effect, popularized by Robert Metcalfe but introduced into economics and business by Theodore Vail, president of Bell Telephone. In 1908, Vail convinced Bell's shareholders to approve his plan to consolidate the thousands of local and regional telephone exchanges by arguing that adding more connections, and people, to the network would increase the network's value exponentially. It did.

Nerdy Tech Economist Derivation

Another way to look at an IoT product is as an intra-network of sensors and an inter-network of external systems connected to provide data to the software-defined product and analytics. The cost of these connections rises linearly, but the resulting value from the data they collect rises exponentially—nicely fitting Metcalfe's law:

$$V \propto n^2$$

or:

$$\text{Value} \propto (\text{number of connections})^2$$

Applying this observation along the IoT Tech Continuum, which gets progressively more networked, derives a different way to explain why the Outcome Economy will be so massive.

The value of an IoT product is proportional to the square of the number of data sources in the system:

$$V(\text{IoT product}) \propto (\text{sources of data})^2$$

The value of an IoT product line is proportional to the square of the number of IoT products in the system:

$$V(\text{IoT product line}) \propto (\text{IoT products})^2$$

The value of an IoT ecosystem is proportional to the square of the number of IoT product lines in the system:

$$V(\text{IoT ecosystem}) \propto (\text{IoT product lines})^2$$

And finally, the value of an Outcome Economy is proportional to the square of the number of IoT ecosystems in the system:

$$V(\text{Outcome Economy}) \propto (\text{IoT ecosystems})^2$$

Using substitution, we get:

$$V(\text{Outcome Economy}) \propto (\text{sources of data})^8$$

Or put another way, the value of an Outcome Economy is *highly* exponentially proportional to the number of data sources within it.

Economies are going to be combinations of Product, Service, and Outcome Economies. Those that are more outcome based will outperform those that are more product or service based. However, the biggest macro-level implication is that the new new economy is all about data—data that are transformed into valuable information by the Internet of Things (Figure 7.9).

THE LONG GAME

This chapter was not meant to be an academic exercise but instead a view into the long game to help you decide what part of the rink to skate to. In the same way that IoT transforms products and companies, it will be equally transformative to economics. Look at your industry through the IoT lens of tech and business coming together to deliver the outcomes your customer wants. Given that

114

Figure 7.9 | IoT technology with support the Outcome Economy

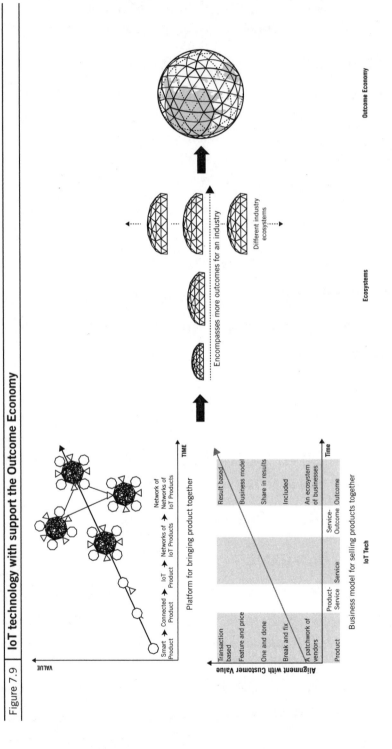

this will unfold over time, use this view to examine your strategic timeline. Once your customer outcome directional vector is defined, it will guide you in all short-term and long-term business decisions that make up your go-to-market strategy, your positioning strategy, and your competitive strategy.

• • •

Next, we are going to look at the operational aspects of making IoT happen in your organization, involving changes that are more tactical than strategic. The next chapter goes through the IoT company, department by department.

CHAPTER 8

YOUR NEW IOT COMPANY— DEPARTMENT BY DEPARTMENT

The technical name for a speed bump is a traffic calming device. Traffic calming originated in the Dutch city of Delft in the late 1960s. Out of fear for the safety of their children, citizens there deliberately pushed benches, tables, and sandboxes partially into the street, creating a vehicular obstacle course to force slower, more responsible driving in their neighborhoods. This and other techniques grew in popularity, reinforcing the notion that the needs of drivers were secondary to the needs of the street's occupants.

Christian Shaffer, a longtime listener of my podcast, reached out to tell me about his company (All Traffic Solutions), which built an IoT version of the radar-sign traffic calming device. You've seen these devices on the road; they show your speed in comparison with the posted speed limit. Although these roadside signs were already successful in slowing down 80 percent of speeders, All Traffic Solutions had a bigger idea.

Its radar sign, a component of its TraffiCloud product line, is an IoT product that not only functions as a calming traffic device, but also provides cities and municipalities with useful information about what is happening on their streets. A sampling of the traffic data with these networked radar sensors produces heat maps that help to identify problem areas, thereby enabling law enforcement to act far more efficiently.

The story Christian shared was about how his company's cool tech and new business model forced a complete reorganization of his company, something he nicely documented in his book, *Customer Success Is Key: How a Small Manufacturer Transformed into an Internet of Things Solution Provider and Unlocked $2 Million in SaaS Revenue*. Whew, the title kind of says it all.

THE TRANSFORMATION

To *effectively* build and sell IoT, the enterprise must transform itself in almost every way it does business. IoT companies like All Traffic Solutions sell differently, market differently, and support their customers differently.

If you consider where value is generated in the IoT, it's all about the software. Marc Andreessen, renowned venture capitalist and inventor of the Netscape browser, stated, "Software is eating the world," and it's no different in IoT. In this case the TraffiCloud solution transforms raw vehicle traffic data into incremental value not available before. So it stands to reason that in order to be successful, an IoT company must become a software company and a data science company. It becomes a consulting company because its relationship with its customer changes, and it becomes a partnering company because it must work with other companies to provide their common customers the outcomes they desire.

At a high level every company will become part of the computer industry; the Silicon Valley is moving to you. Operationally, these changes affect every department: engineering, data, manufacturing, marketing, sales, support and maintenance, business development, HR, and legal. The IoT enterprise is updated and reorganized to take advantage of the two major trends galvanized by the Internet of Things: the IoT Tech Continuum (Chapter 5) and the IoT Business Model Continuum (Chapter 3). In this chapter, we will discuss the operational changes needed, department by department, to effectively develop and sell an IoT product.

ENGINEERING

New intellectual property (know-how) must be developed to build an IoT product. Software development and data science must become core competencies of every IoT company. They should not be subcontracted, but if this is necessary to move forward in the short term, ensure there is a plan to bring the intellectual property back in-house.

Some of my clients have had zero software developers, while others have had over 10,000. Whether hiring new or transferring from within, the key is to find the *right* talent. In either case, we need software developers with experience in leveraging Internet services and products through APIs.

Then there's the issue of working within fast-moving environments. Within organizations making physical products, there will likely be in-house embedded programming talent, but often their cadence matches the cadence of their hardware counterparts, and that's not fast enough. Embedded software in the IoT product will be refreshed many times every hardware development cycle. Beyond embedded programming skills, IoT companies must also become apt in mobile development, back-end server development, and cloud development.

Instead of employing a traditional cascading waterfall model, IoT engineering teams must enact the agile development philosophy. The IoT product manager has a gusher of customer data coming in daily, which is a new and major source of input for product improvement. To capitalize on this golden resource, it's necessary to be able to rapidly iterate and update the IoT product's software.

IT/OT

Discussing the technicalities of the IT and OT networks (see Chapter 13) is easier than deciding where the resources go in the organization. This combined group could be a part of the existing IT organization, but the fit isn't great given the group's main responsibilities of maintaining computers systems, onboarding mobile devices, establishing VPNs, etc.

Or it could be that IT, or at least the relevant part of IT, is organizationally folded under the operations group. Some organizations will have an existing operations group to ensure their products (like the IoT bucket wheel excavator or smart grid) are always operating. But I'm not sure that makes sense either, since we are predominantly dealing with networking technology, whereas the traditional domain of the operations group is business operations.

Bringing these groups together has other challenges as well. Besides the obvious political ones, there is also the issue of where they sit on the P&L. IT is a cost center, and operations is part of a revenue center. It's a little like mixing oil and water.

Each situation needs to be judged separately, but the best organizational structure is to bring together the relevant parts of the IT organization and the operations organization to make them part of engineering. Since a big part of this type of work is a systems engineering play, and its part of the "product," bringing together the IT and OT engineering resources makes sense. It may also make sense to throw in a little data science when you are at it, although as we will see, there's also a strong argument to create a separate data department that builds and maintains this new corporate asset; and incidentally this is an asset that will start appearing on the balance sheet more frequently.

MANUFACTURING

For IoT it could be argued that manufacturing, whether done in-house or outsourced, should be part of engineering. Software is not made with atoms and therefore can be iterated upon much faster than physical products and hardware. Aligning the cadence of software development and hardware development is a challenge for the IoT company, as is the need for manufacturing to be data driven by the customer. It could continue to be a separate organization, but operationally, it would be best to fold manufacturing into engineering.

MARKETING

I'm a fan of data-driven marketing, both for inbound marketing and for outbound marketing. When I was VP of marketing, we measured the cost and the return on the investment of all our demand-generation instruments. Even before we had web analytics, my team was measuring the cost per lead, and when we could, we traced it to the cost per sale. Today, doing A/B split testing for SEO and quantifying social media is more of the norm, and it's this kind of data-driven thinking that needs to be imprinted on the DNA of the marketing org of the IoT company.

IoT improves marketing with data, lots of data. IoT data-driven marketing begins with building and then analyzing the utility and usability models of your product. If you remember from Chapter 2, a utility model captures what a product is used for and a usability model captures how the product is being used. Marketing resources are required to visualize and interpret the data for both inbound and outbound marketing.

Inbound Marketing

Software usability models have been around for years and started with old-school application code. Before everything was networked, it was difficult to get this type of data unless done in a focus group, where users would be watched behind one-way glass and the data would be pulled off the computer after the fact for analysis. Fast-forward a couple of decades and the craft of software usability models has really advanced in the high-stakes field of e-commerce sites. Knowing how the visitor navigates the site is of paramount concern when it comes to conversion—that is, how many people on a particular web page, laid out in a particular way, make a purchase or reach different goals. Making the page easier to use will lead to more sales.

Similar analytics and visualization tools can now be applied to physical products via the usability model and the more sophisticated utility model. When employed by product marketing, these models are used to make existing products better and to create new products from the ideas found within. Data from these models can also be used to prioritize product features and updates and to establish more sophisticated market segmentation and positioning. If the manager knows how the customer is using the product and how the customer makes money, tying the two together results in accurate value pricing and ROI calculations. Think about that. This requires a specific type of inbound marketing organization, one that is capable of getting down and dirty with the bits.

Outbound Marketing

While the customer data are quantified for inbound marketing, they are also qualified for outbound marketing. The same utility and usability models can be used by outbound marketing to craft highly targeted messaging. IoT data-driven outbound marketing programs can produce hyperpersonalized contextualized messaging based on customer use cases and can be used to predict when to send a message to sell, for example, a needed expendable.

Remember the tire example of the product-service business model in Chapter 3? Whether or not that tire's data are sold as an information product, the data can be used by marketing communications and sales. In this case, the tire is a renewable, and since we know when the tread is getting low, we can communicate with the fleet manager to let him or her know that the tires on truck X will become unsafe in two months, and if the company buys replacements right now, we'll provide a 20 percent discount.

SALES

The evolution of the business model through its continuum (see Chapter 3) will completely change sales. It will change what is sold, how it's sold, and to whom it's sold (Figure 8.1).

Figure 8.1	The changing role of sales	
	PRODUCT	**IOT PRODUCT**
What is sold	A tool with features that solve point problems	Outcome the customer needs
How it's sold	Solution-based selling	Outcome-based selling
To whom it's sold	User/department	User/business
Value delivered	Indirect—a means to an end result	Direct—the end outcome

At the core of these changes is the IoT product's ability to quantify what is important to the customer. With the ability to measure customer success comes the ability to get paid based on this success. Salespeople, however, are "coin-operated." Once the sale has been made, it's on to the next one. And that's OK; it's how their compensation is structured today. But if this mindset and compensation structure does not change in the IoT world, we are squandering a great opportunity, or should I say, a more profitable opportunity, that also just happens to be more valuable to the customer. It is this thinking that changes everything. Let me explain.

Instead of looking for pain points, problems to solve, the focus should change to delivering outcomes, the outcomes the customer wants. At the highest level, the customer wants higher profitability: reducing costs by improving operational efficiency or increasing revenue by improving operational performance, or both. How this is done depends on the desired outcome, but it always starts by aligning your company's interests with the interests of your customer.

Aligning Interests

If this sounds more like a consultative relationship than a transactional one, it is. It's a long-term play that will continue to pay dividends. The logical conclusion to such a relationship is to align both parties' business models. This then explicitly aligns the interests of the buy and sell sides of the relationship, removing all indirection and fluff. This shifts the transaction away from competing on price to competing on value and profit.

When a salesperson sells a widget, he or she is selling something of indirect value, something that works with other widgets to produce an outcome. It is sold therefore to the operator or user of the widget and probably the person's boss. When a salesperson sells an outcome, it is of direct value, value that can be measured and related to how it affects profit. Not only does this sale include the user or operator, but it's also of interest to the person responsible for the business—the owner of the P&L.

Composition of the Salesforce

This shift to outcomes dictates a similarly profound transformation in the composition of the salesforce. This requires a different type of salesperson with a different skill set. It is most reminiscent of the business services offered by companies like IBM, which transformed from selling products to selling services. The sales organization for the IoT company will be more like a services organization: business consultants working with clients to improve their business and being paid based on the results. And through this intense focus on the customer's business, sales will discover new opportunities to provide value that can be monetized as a product or a service or an outcome.

Customer Success

The change from a product focus to an outcome focus generally makes a stop at the service business model along the way. To support the service business model, an ongoing relationship with the customer must be established to ensure success. Since the service business model perpetually comes up for renewal, the customer must be repeatedly sold to ensure the customer renews. No longer once and done, sales needs to be intentional and proactive. The customer success department in sales is responsible for ensuring that the customer gets the most out of the product and that the customer is continuously satisfied. Tools to monitor product use and performance are available, but this relationship must be established and nurtured by adding consultative value.

This group can be organizationally structured in different ways. Christian Shaffer's title is Director of Customer Success, heading up a separate department for the previously mentioned All Traffic Solutions. Others will make it a part of an existing sales organization, separating the two sales functions (hunting and maintenance), and yet others will change the job descriptions of all salespeople to include these responsibilities. Whatever the structure, the return is maximizing customer lifetime value and minimizing churn.

It's important to remember that this function supports the service business model, blending traditional sales and consulting. When the outcome business model is deployed, this organization and all sales will transition almost completely to business consultation.

SUPPORT AND MAINTENANCE

Unlike with traditional products, the relationship with the customer doesn't abruptly end once the product is sold. The IoT product, with help from its OTA (over-the-air) update mechanism, continues to delight customer with new product updates, new services, and security patches.

By using IoT tech and the data it provides, support and maintenance is undergoing a transformation from reactive and preventive to proactive to predictive and, finally, to the promised land of prescriptive. Getting there requires a shift from physical support to cyber support. Cyber support actuates the product remotely to mechanically repair the problem or to deliver software updates and patches. This transition requires a different kind of support personnel, who, like all other employees, will be data driven and will be users of analytics.

Although an increasing amount of support will be done virtually, the need for sending personnel into the field with tools will not go away. With analytics this process will become more effi-cient by sending out the right personnel who know the problem in advance and take with them the right tools and parts for the repair.

BUSINESS DEVELOPMENT

In IoT, no one company can do it all. Whether it's IBM, GE, or Intel, every company needs to partner with others in order to deliver on IoT's promise. No company has the horizontal breadth of technology to go from sensor to analytics, and no company has enough domain knowledge in every vertical needed to deliver a deep enough solution.

IoT technology enables physical products from different ven-dors to work together on behalf of the customer, but it's going to be business that drives the corporate relationships needed to pay for the connections. The end goal is an ecosystem, but partner-ships can start out less formally through business development. Using outcomes, determine who would ideally be in your ecosys-tem and reach out with biz dev to establish initial relationships based on sales and marketing and then development.

Ecosystems will become increasingly more important, not only to fill tech gaps but to strategically position your company within your industry. Consolidation will not come down to which companies offer the best technical solution, but to which compa-nies offer the best business solution. Consortia such as the Open Connectivity Foundation, Industrial Internet Consortium, and others are of strategic importance not because of their technical framework but because of the business framework they provide. This starts by clearing intellectual property barriers between mem-ber companies and establishing common business models to com-mercialize the ecosystem.

Ecosystems start and keep operating through the efforts of business development.

DATA DEPARTMENT

The data department has two functions—science and analysis. Data scientists need to be proficient in statistics and programming. Data analysts must be proficient in statistics and be able to look into the numbers to tell business stories about them—stories related to value. The skills needed can be separated into two sets. Skills in the first set are technical and could comfortably live in engineering. Skills in the second set are business focused and could easily live in the line of business or the CIO's organization.

In the midterm to long term, however, I believe every organization would be best served spinning up a separate data department. This data department is aligned with value creation and as such should be led by a chief data officer, to consolidate the strategy for data collection, data aggregation, and data analysis.

Whatever the reporting structure, this department is critical to every enterprise, so developing the "special sauce" (data recipes) shouldn't be outsourced; it needs to reside in-house, along with the rest of the company's IP. Data science and analytics must become a core competency of every IoT company. I believe so strongly in the need and value of this vocation that I'm encouraging my son, Chase, to consider data analytics as a career path. He's in high school, and like me when I was in high school, he doesn't have a clear direction yet. Data science and analytics will become fundamental to all industries, offering plenty of options and flexibility.

HUMAN RESOURCES

Not only does a data-driven company have to recruit new types of talent, such as software developers and data scientists, but it also needs to train all employees on data-driven thinking and with new skills (see Figure 8.2). As we've seen, how data are collected and consumed within an IoT organization is the source of a major competitive advantage. While IoT opens up new positions, it also makes others obsolete or redundant. This underlines the importance of an employee training program, to augment certain jobs and to retrain employees for others.

As new software development and data science employees are introduced into the organization, it will be HR's responsibility to manage and nurture the cultural changes that will develop. It's not realistic nor is it authentic for a traditional manufacturing company to turn into a Twitter or Google, but it should look to high tech for examples of how the company will need to culturally change to accommodate these new types of employees. They will be in high demand, so the new IoT company must create an environment that is competitive and familiar to high-tech employees. These changes can seem overwhelming, but they start slow and

Figure 8.2	**New skill sets required**

1. **Application developers**—to develop software-defined product application
2. **Engineers and programmers**—to manage networking, cloud, database, sensors
3. **Security professionals**—to secure web, cloud, networking, system
4. **Data scientists/analysts**—to create and interpret analytics
5. **Solution architects**—to develop models with domain knowledge and advanced analytics skills
6. **UX designers**—to incorporate information into design and experience
7. **Big data marketers**—to synthesize analytics and package it for inbound/outbound programs
8. **Business consultants**—to work at all levels of customer's organization to add value to business

start small, coalescing around the new competencies of software development and data science.

LEGAL

Although data are an asset, they are also a legal liability that needs to be managed. Data liabilities around privacy, physical safety, contractual agreements, financial losses, and brand reputation require a different set of legal skills, ones that may be developed in-house or found externally.

• • •

Now that we have gone through each department of the IoT company, we move on to requirements. Since IoT product requirements are about more than just the product, the next chapter takes a 360-degree approach to consider all aspects of the IoT company's business when defining its product's requirements.

DEFINING YOUR IOT PRODUCT'S REQUIREMENTS

Cooking the perfect steak is as much a science as it is a culinary art. As such, the frying pan makes for a fun example of an IoT product. This chapter will show you, step by step, how to develop your IoT products requirements. The commercial IoT example used in the chapter was chosen because it's also applicable to consumer IoT. This chapter serves the secondary purpose of reviewing a lot of the material in this book by practically putting it into action.

COOKING THE PERFECT STEAK WITH IOT

The three characteristics that define the perfect steak are flavor, texture, and juiciness. By understanding the science of cooking muscle, we can quantify each characteristic into a mathematical recipe.

Searing a steak serves two purposes: killing the surface-based pathogens and creating texture. The golden texture is created by the Maillard reaction, in which sugars and amino acids combine in a chemical reaction to create new flavorful compounds, similar to what happens when bread is toasted. To achieve the Maillard reaction, the external surface of meat must reach a temperature of 350°F.

The internal structure and texture of meat changes when the proteins that make up the muscle fibers change shape as they're heated. This "denature" temperature is different for each protein. The best flavor and texture for steak is generally considered to be when the temperature is hot enough to denature myosin proteins but not hot enough to denature actin proteins. This bookends the internal temperature to the specific range of 125°–150°F (see Table 9.1).

Table 9.1	Cooking Meat by Temperature	
	Rare	130°F
	Medium rare	135°F
	Medium	145°F
	Medium well	160°F
	Well done	170°F

To produce a tender and juicy steak, the chef must break down the collagen, that is, the fibers and ligaments that make up the cow's connective tissue. This begins at 140°F and ends at 190°F; however, there is a nuanced balance. The process of melting collagen into gelatin gives steak a creamy texture and more flavor, but the process squeezes out liquid, making it less moist and chewier. To maintain the juiciness, the internal temperature can't rise too quickly.

Stovetop Precision

Food is cooked by temperature; however, unlike the oven, stovetop cooking currently does not measure temperature, and so frying food is a matter of experience or guesswork. Oven recipes are quantitative: "Cook at 350° for 20 minutes." Stove-top recipes are qualitative: "Cook at medium heat for 20 minutes." The IoT frying pan changes this.

The IoT frying pan, consisting of a cooking surface and app, must precisely control both the external and internal temperature of the steak, over time, to cook it to perfection. The frying pan determines the exterior and interior temperature of the meat through sensors and analytics, and the software application guides the cook through the recipe, step by step, providing instructions on how to adjust the temperature, synchronized with when to add different ingredients.

A 360-DEGREE VIEW

The IoT requirements doc defines your product's IoT-related functionality. Traditionally a product's requirements are synonymous with its customer's requirements, but for an IoT product, it's different. Because of its nature and capabilities, we take a 360-degree approach to requirements, considering not only the customer but other key aspects of the business as well. This is a top-down approach that starts with value and then identifies the model requirements, the application requirements, and the analytics requirements needed to satisfy the IoT value proposition and other business goals.

I've been on both sides of this one. When I was a developer, it drove me crazy to start with mushy requirements only to have them rewritten as I was coding. When I was a CEO, I forced the discipline of a stringent requirements process, and everyone benefited. Having said that, it's important to recognize that there is always room for research in tech, so you can't lock things down so tightly that there isn't any room for innovation beyond what the customer is asking for. But depending on the stage of your company, I'd say little room—especially early on. Until you're at breakeven, relying on customers more than hunches is a sensible goal. A clear, concise list of requirements, vetted by prospects, is gold.

Like the business plan, the first pass of the IoT requirements document is written based on internal thinking, after ideation and before anything has been developed (see Figure 9.1). There may be an IoT lab for experimenting, but the software, firmware, and hardware of the IoT product should not be started in earnest until this first pass of the requirements doc is complete (see Chapter 10).

Once written, the IoT requirements document is not set in stone. Quite the contrary. As part of the lean development process, it will be evaluated and changed at each development milestone by interacting with prospective customers, partners, and internal stakeholders. Think of this living document as a compass, pointing in the right direction but not dictating an exact path. The further into the development cycle, the clearer the path, refined by different stakeholder interactions along the way. Of course, the IoT requirements process is intended to augment your existing requirements process, not replace it.

An exhaustive list of requirements for the IoT frying pan will not be developed here—that wouldn't be practical or any more useful. Instead the focus will be on how to come up with the different types of requirements.

Figure 9.1	**Requirements during preproduction**

Requirements 1.0		2.0		3.0		4.0	5.0	
Preproduction							Production	
Concept	Ideation		POC		Prototype/Pilot	MVP		

KEY REQUIREMENTS TO CONSIDER

Defining our IoT requirements sets into motion a process (shown in Figure 9.2) by which we examine the key aspects of our business, asking three questions at every step along the way:

- What data do we need for our model?

- What do we need our application to do?

- What do we need from our data analytics?

Figure 9.2	The 360-degree requirements process

Examine five key aspects of the business:	For each step determine:
• Step 1: Value	• Model requirements
• Step 2: Monetization	• Application requirements
• Step 3: Outcome	• Analytics requirements
• Step 4: Industry	
• Step 5: Operations	

Model Requirements

We start by asking, what information do we need to support our model? (See Chapter 11.) And knowing that the information is created by transforming an IoT product's data, the question quickly becomes, what data do we need in order to produce that information? These are the data we need to collect, influencing the sensors we will source (buy) and the external systems we will connect to over the Internet. These data are transformed by the application and analytics.

Application Requirements

The application (see Chapter 11) is the product's logic, the product's functionality. It is the human interface with the customer and end user, and it is also the cyber interface with sensors and external systems, ultimately orchestrating data to and from the model and analytics. These requirements define what software needs to be developed, not how the software is developed nor where on the computing fabric (embedded, fog, mobile, or cloud) it resides.

Analytics Requirements

To develop our analytics (see Chapter 15), we cycle through the key aspects of our business and ask ourselves, what do we need to do to the data to make them valuable? We consider three classes of analytics: analytics to derive insights about the past, analytics to make decisions in the present, and analytics to make predictions about the future. When interpreted technically, this will influence the application architecture, the development environment, the databases used, and of course the analytics packages we need to interface with.

KEY BUSINESS AREAS TO CONSIDER

To define our requirements, we step through five key areas of our business, one at a time:

- **Step 1: Value.** What do we require to make our product better, operate our product better, support our product better, and make new products? This step begins with value modeling.

- **Step 2: Monetization.** What do we require to support our business model and to look into the business model of our customer? And is there anything we should plan for today to support future business model needs as they evolve along the IoT Business Model Continuum?

- **Step 3: Outcome.** What do we require to reach the outcome the customer wants? This means leveraging external players, because we can't do it alone.

- **Step 4: Industry.** What do we require to support our strategy? What is needed to position our company in the right direction and to give us a competitive edge?

- **Step 5: Operations.** What information do we require to improve the operations of our company? A successful IoT product takes into account the internal needs we have for every department in our company, and in the process, it helps create a successful IoT company.

Security

Security requirements should be considered horizontally. It is not a separate step; instead security requirements are defined within each of the five requirements steps. Beyond being part of the original design (security by design), we also consider security during each milestone of the development process. Security is discussed in more detail in Chapter 16 in the context of risk management.

REQUIREMENTS FOR THE IOT FRYING PAN

We will cook the perfect steak to define the requirements of the IoT frying pan, cycling through the five business areas to define the model, application, and analytics requirements. We finish by consolidating the requirements into the first pass of the IoT requirements document that, with the first pass of the business plan, is presented to prospects.

For illustrative purposes the requirements for the IoT frying pan will consider both commercial and consumer applications. This will probably yield a Frankensteinlike product that has too many commercial features for the cook and too many consumer features for the professional chef (generally referred to as cook for the rest of this chapter), but that's OK—it will have just the right number of features for this chapter.

Step 1: Value

The first step in defining the requirements of the IoT frying pan (see Figure 9.3) is to consider the incremental value it generates. We've discussed value modeling extensively in the book with examples that deliberately focused on only one of the four methods of value generation. In the 360-degree method, we will consider value generation from all perspectives: making a better frying pan, operating the frying pan better, supporting the frying pan better, and creating new information products related to the frying pan.

We start by qualifying the value proposition of the IoT frying pan: *Fry food perfectly every time.*

| Figure 9.3 | **The IoT frying pan** |

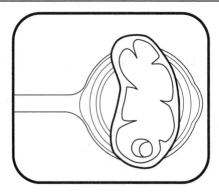

Model Requirements

We then quantify the value proposition to create the cybermodel with value modeling. Frying each type of food is a function of pan temperature and cooking time as well as food weight and volume. The exact mathematical function of the model is not our responsibility, but ideally we should be able to identify which data need to be collected. The high-level model for frying food is:

$$\text{Frying} = f(\text{food type, temp, time, weight, volume})$$

These five variables need to be directly collected as data or calculated from data for each recipe we offer. We also need a utility and usability model for our IoT frying pan.

Application Requirements

The recipe for cooking the perfect steak, or any other food for that matter, is to control the variables you can and measure the ones you can't. For the IoT frying pan we will have a different application for each steak recipe; in fact, we'll have applications for every recipe. The application must guide the cook through the recipe to control cooking time and temperature, as well as manage ingredients and the pan. There may also be an opportunity for customer support. The application does take the cook through the recipe, but the support of a live expert support chef to walk the cook through a particularly tricky part of the recipe may be worth paying for.

Analytics Requirements

Our analytics requirements span analysis about the future, present, and past. For future analytics we need to correlate our recipes with results in order to make predictions. In this case we need to correlate each recipe with how well the meal turned out. Since this is subjective, we will need to add another application requirement: a survey asking the cook how the recipe turned out. The analytics requirements are to correlate the variables we control in our value model with each different survey; i.e., how did the grilled teriyaki steak recipes turn out when the variables for food type, temperature, time, weight, and the volume calculation had these values? This will enable us to improve our recipes and predict how the food will turn out under different conditions (different variable combinations).

In the present we need to analyze, in real time, the internal temperature of our food. Just as for cooking a steak, this is critical for any recipe. It must use food type, surface temperature, volume, and weight for this analysis.

For analyzing the past we combine our knowledge about pan usage and recipes to classify our recipes beyond just their ingredients. For example, recipes might be categorized by most popular by demographic (geography, cook age, . . .), fastest to prepare, cheapest to make, etc. This same information can be used as the basis for a recommendation engine.

Requirements for step 1 are summarized in Table 9.2.

Table 9.2	**Summary of Step 1 Requirements**		
	Models and Data to Collect	**Application**	**Analytics**
Step 1	For each recipe: Frying = f(food type, temp, time, weight, volume) Utility model Usability model	Different application for each recipe Walk cook through each recipe on mobile device Survey cook about how recipe turned out Chat or use audio or video communications for support	Build "results" model linking variables to results of survey Estimate internal temperature of food Descriptive analytics operating on usage models Recipe hyperclassification (for recommendation engine)

Step 2: Monetization

The second step in the requirements definition is to consider the information you need to support your business model, not only on launch day, but also as it evolves over time on the IoT Business Model Continuum. Related is the business model of your customer. How are your customers paid? Can you measure components of their business model to help them get paid? Can you measure or calculate any of their KPIs? Is there anything else you can measure that can save the customer money or make the customer money? And finally, what is your competition's business model? Is there any information your product can produce that would provide it with a competitive advantage in this dimension?

To start we ask ourselves, how are we going to sell the frying pan today and in the future? Let's go through each of the five stages of the IoT Business Model Continuum to see what makes sense for our business and the business of our customer.

Product Business Model

In the product business model, we are just selling the frying pan and including recipes, but like the Tesla example in Chapter 2, we will periodically provide new upgrades (recipes) to give it that new car (pan) smell.

Product-Service Business Model

The product-service business model is similar except we sell the frying pan plus we sell optional services, or information products. We've already discussed one information service, and that's recipes. And if we sell recipes, which ones should we sell? The best ones, of course. Perhaps we provide a list of the most popular recipes and let our cooks decide which ones to download. We could also analyze the in-kitchen ingredients inventory to determine which recipes can be made without having to go to the store. Or we could sell specialized recipes, say for diabetics or for athletes. We can either produce all these recipes ourselves or use popular recipes from the web.

What are our requirements so far? In the first two business models, we need a way to upload new recipes to the application, dictating an over-the-air (OTA) update mechanism. We also need a way to communicate with the cook, so another requirement is to capture his or her e-mail address and preferences and a method to send out e-mails. We need analytics to determine which are the best recipes and review our ingredients inventory to see what's on hand. And we need to hook into certain websites to pull out recipes.

Service Business Model

Now let's look at the frying pan–as–a–service business model. Here we are not selling the hardware; instead we are selling the act of cooking—the service the frying pan provides. This business model could be monetized by KPIs of interest to the commercial kitchen such as the number of times the pan is used or the overall time the frying pan is used. Our requirements will be to measure both.

Service-Outcome Business Model

Let's now consider the service-outcome business model. What is the outcome in this case, and can we charge for it? As opposed to the usage of the pan that's measured for the service model, the desired outcome is a completed meal, so we need to keep track of the number of completed meals. Generally, in this business model, money flows in partly as a service fee and partly as a percentage of how much was saved or how much more money was made.

Starting with efficiency, the variables involved are saving on ingredients, energy, and the cook's time. I'm not sure saving on ingredients makes sense for the business model, but in general it will be useful to assign costs to the ingredients used, which has model, application, and analytics ramifications. Measuring energy consumption will involve the time the pan is in use and energy costs. And the cook's time is a little broader than just pan cooking time, so it too can be a requirement for the application.

Looking at the top line for the professional chef, we recognize that making more revenue means completing more meals over time or charging more per meal. We are already measuring usage time, so we should also count the number of meals completed.

Outcome Business Model

The requirements for the outcome of completing a meal have been covered in the previous business model, but the next step, step 3, digs much further into delivering the outcome in a broader sense, so let's wait until then.

Requirements for step 2 are summarized in Table 9.3.

Step 3: Outcome

The third step in defining your product's requirements forces you to look beyond your product and broaden your thinking to include everything involved in helping your customers achieve their desired outcome. What do the customers do with your product, and what other products do your customers buy, related or unrelated to yours, to reach their goals? Determine what data you can capture, features you should add, and analytics that should be performed, in order to interface with other products and services that would help customers achieve their outcome.

People don't want frying pans; they are a means to an end. They want what the frying pan does. In this case, what your customers want are meals, preferably healthy and delicious meals, and

Table 9.3	**Summary of Step 2 Requirements**

	Models and Data to Collect	Application	Analytics
Step 2	Recipe popularity Length of time the pan is used Number of completed meals Ingredients recipe model Customer ingredients inventory model	Create specialized recipes Capture e-mail addresses and customer info Send e-mails to customers Connect to recipe websites or online recipe data services to get external recipes Use OTA update mechanism Monitor length of time and number of times the pan is used Connect to internal ingredients inventory (if there is one) Connect to grocery store data service to get the price and inventory of each ingredient Connect to utility data service to get energy cost Track the amount of time the recipe is being interacted with (cook's total time spent)	Determine most popular recipes from the past Calculate cost of each ingredient used in each recipe Do a kitchen inventory analysis Calculate cost of each recipe

let's say they want meals that can be prepared quickly. What else in addition to your frying pan is needed to contribute to this outcome of a healthy and fast meal . . . present and future?

Let's pull back and look at the sequence of events that must occur to achieve this outcome. Whether for the professional in the restaurant or the amateur in the kitchen, the overall pipeline for this outcome is:

Shopping —→ Preparation —→ Cooking —→ Eating —→ Cleanup

To get that great steak dinner, all the ingredients must be bought. The steak must be prepped, along with any side dishes. Next is where the frying pan and other cookware come in—to cook the meal. The meal is eaten, and then everything must be cleaned, put away, and made available to be used again.

When looking at requirements from the outcome perspective, we need to examine all the products and services that are part of the pipeline. To achieve the outcome, there will be value in connecting the frying pan to other products and services in the pipeline. Of course this example is only for illustrative purposes. Think about your product, the overall pipeline it's part of and what other products your product should connect to, to deliver the desired outcome.

Everything you can do to integrate your product, in this case the IoT frying pan, into the overall pipeline, the more value your frying pan will ultimately provide. Let's look at each sequence in the pipeline in our search for requirements.

Shopping

Our IoT frying pan could build a shopping list of the ingredients needed to make all the planned recipes that week. This requires that our application hook into a shopping application or connect directly to a grocery store service to buy the ingredients online and have them delivered.

Preparation

During the prep stage the chef may want to have the frying pan connected to a kitchen scale or other kitchen appliances to help streamline the cooking process.

Cooking

During the cooking stage, the frying pan will not be the only cookware used. To provide synchronization or an exchange of information, we will need to connect to other smart cookware that are part of our product line or, later, the product line of partners.

Eating

You wouldn't expect IoT to be involved in the act of eating, but funny enough, it can be. This is a bit of a stretch, but if our value statement were to include weight loss, our frying pan could connect to smart cutlery to monitor and potentially correct eating pace and portion control. Yes, there is connected cutlery for sale . . . at least for now.

Cleanup

Cleanup is the last phase. Connecting to a dishwasher could have benefit, and so too could connecting to a dish-cleaning service, where dirty plates, flatware, and cookware are picked up and replaced with clean ones. Logistics aside, who doesn't like room service?

Some of these outcome examples are a little far-fetched . . . or are they? In any case, that's not the point. The point is the methodology—the thinking. Looking at outcomes reveals the big picture and helps identify the connections that can be made between your IoT product and other IoT products, applications, and data services.

Requirements for step 3 are summarized in Table 9.4.

Table 9.4	Summary of Step 3 Requirements		
	Models and Data to Collect	**Application**	**Analytics**
Step 3		Connect to one or more online shopping apps to order ingredients	
		Connect to grocery store service to order ingredients	
		Connect to online kitchen scale and other connected kitchen appliances	
		Connect to other Internet cookware	
		Connect to Internet gadgets	
		Connect to housecleaning service	

Step 4: Industry

The fourth step in gathering requirements has to do with your industry and how it will change over time. During the previous step, we looked at other products; in this step, we look at other organizations. These are organizations we will work with (and against) in order to increase overall value for our customers. Which companies are or can be part of your supply chain? Which companies are or can be part of your distribution? Which companies should you work with to deliver the outcome your customer wants?

To start, use the thinking in Chapter 5 to identify your company's potential partners, competitors, and consolidators and then determine your product requirements in order to establish relationships with key partners and consolidators and fend off competitors. Undoubtedly platforms and ecosystems will also come into play. The goal with this set of requirements is to anticipate what can be done now to position your company toward a more competitive place in the future.

Partners

Which companies should we interface with to make our IoT frying pan a success today and tomorrow? Together we may not be able to deliver the full outcome, but partnerships are the step to ecosystems, which deliver outcomes. Dominant players that offer kitchen appliances or even gadgets, used before, during, or after the cooking phase, are our partnership targets. What would be required to interface with their products or services or platforms?

Competitors

Are there requirements we should include that would give us an advantage over our competitors—current or future? In the case of the IoT frying pan, a direct competitor is the connected food thermometer, which in many ways simplifies the act of measuring the internal temperature of our steak. Stick it in and measure. So perhaps it would be advantageous to provide a disproportionate number of recipes for meals where a food thermometer would be difficult to use. Focusing on recipes for one-pan dishes, such as pasta, beef stroganoff, or stews, would be one way to positively position the frying pan through the requirements definition.

Consolidators

Now let's think longer term and bigger picture. Which organizations could end up being the consolidators? That is, which companies or groups have the size and focus to make the investments required to offer a platform and ecosystem for your industry vertical? In this case, since the kitchen is a subset of the home, major players in the smart home industry would be a good place to start. At this time, Amazon, Google, Apple, and Samsung are all vying to own the home ecosystem along with dozens of other companies that offer smart home point products.

Consortia are the other place to look for consolidators and ecosystem providers. Sometimes backed by large corporations and sometimes not, organizations like the Open Connectivity Foundation are trying to establish their own connected home platform through their member libraries and development environments.

Whether corporate or not, what is required to "work" with these consolidators? In all cases, working with these consolidators means supporting their IoT platform, API, and development environment.

This is a closed game. Partnerships lead to ecosystems that deliver outcomes. Ecosystems have finite space. And organizations that aren't competitive today may become your biggest competitors. In all cases, whether getting closer to partners and consolidators or getting further away from competitors, the exercise is the same: what are the model, application, and analytics requirements needed to support your strategy?

Requirements for step 4 are summarized in Table 9.5.

Table 9.5	**Summary of Step 4 Requirements**

	Models and Data to Collect	Application	Analytics
Step 4	Must interface with chosen platform	Interface with platform (general, home, or smart kitchen) of choice Connect to other connected appliances and gadgets Focus recipes on non-thermometer-friendly dishes	Must interface with chosen platform

Step 5: Operations

Now we consider requirements from an internal point of view. The fifth and final step in defining your IoT product requirements is related to improving your organization. In this step we ask, what information can our IoT product provide that would improve the operations of our organization?—which, by the way, has the virtuous effect of improving the product. To define these requirements, we examine each department with an eye to improving its operational efficiency and adding value to the product.

For our IoT frying pan to be successful, our company must be successful in how we make the frying pan, sell the frying pan, and support the frying pan. What information can our IoT product relay back to our company to improve operations? Well, let's cycle through and see.

Engineering

In addition to being used to provide customers with new recipes (step 2), engineering requires an OTA mechanism to update the pan with new software updates and security patches. Also, build and use utility and usability models to innovate product and potentially invent others.

Manufacturing

Our utility model (what the frying pan is used for) and usability model (how the frying pan is being used) in conjunction with support data can influence manufacturing quality and costs. For example, if the product is consistently breaking from being used for an unintended but popular purpose, the weak part can be manufactured differently in order to strengthen it.

Marketing

Inbound marketing is greatly improved by knowing which features have the highest priority and which products should be developed next. Product management will use descriptive analytics in conjunction with the utility model and usability model to analyze how to improve the product and how to extend into a product line with new frying products, completely new cookware, or information products.

For outbound marketing, including branding and demand generation, it would be useful to know the demographics of our customers to identify our target audience. It would be useful to know how often the people in our audience use our product and which recipes they choose. We require this information both in aggregate form for broad communication and individually per customer for direct communication.

Sales

Sales could benefit from knowing which recipes are being used by individual customers in order to up-sell them expendables, which in this case are the ingredients used to make their recipes. Heavy users, whom we can identify, can be up-sold more advanced services, such as educational products and specialized weekly recipes based on region or diet.

Support and Maintenance

To be masters at support, we need to know how our customers use and what they do with the frying pan (covered with the usability and utility models) along with the ability to access the frying pan remotely and put it in diagnostic mode in case something fails.

Data Department

No specific requirements are needed except to model and capture data in a way that allows us to use off-the-shelf or open-source analytics packages with the minimal amount of integration code.

Legal

Is there any information we should capture or should not capture about the product and its users to be in compliance with laws, regulations, and certifications? What risks can we mitigate with the data that we capture? For the IoT frying pan, there may be PII (personal identifiable information) restrictions if sold in certain countries, so we need our application to clearly get the consent of the cooks to use their info. For liability reasons we may want to keep track of any dangerous ways the product could be used. For example, black box–like functionality could be used to track instances when the pan got too hot by being left on for too long.

Requirements for step 5 are summarized in Table 9.6.

Table 9.6	Summary of Step 5 Requirements

	Models and Data to Collect	Application	Analytics
Step 5	Utility model Usability model Customer demographics model Ingredients recipe model	Use OTA update mechanism Collect demographic info Remote access Include diagnostic mode Get consent to use customer data Black box–like functionality	Use utility and usability models to improve design and identify future products Number of times the pan is used and its frequency of use Recipe popularity Recipe usage

Bringing It All Together

The summation of all the requirements for our model, application, and analytics from the five different "views" of your business (shown in Table 9.7) is the first version of your IoT requirements document. As discussed in the next chapter, this list will be added to and reprioritized each time it is presented to prospects during the preproduction phase of development.

Significant technology purchasing decisions should only be made after producing these 360-degree requirements. In the "Development Order and Dependencies" section in the next chapter, we discuss how these requirements are prioritized while making technology purchasing decisions.

Table 9.7 | **Summary of All Requirements**

Models and Data to Collect	Application	Analytics
For each recipe: Frying = f(food type, temp, time, weight, volume)	Develop a different application for each recipe	Build "results" model linking variables to results of survey
Utility model	Walk cook through each recipe on mobile device	Estimate internal temperature of food
Usability model	Survey cook about how recipe turned out	Descriptive analytics operating on usage models
Recipe popularity	Chat or use audio or video communications for support	Recipe hyperclassification (for recommendation engine)
Length of time the pan is used	Create specialized recipes	Determine most popular recipes from the past
Number of completed meals	Capture e-mail addresses and customer info	Recipe usage
Ingredients recipe model	Send e-mails to customers	Calculate cost of each ingredient used in each recipe
Customer ingredients inventory model	Connect to recipe websites or online recipe data services to get external recipes	Do a kitchen inventory analysis
Must interface with chosen platform	Use OTA update mechanism	Calculate cost of each recipe
Customer demographics model	Monitor length of time and number of times the pan is used	Must interface with chosen platform
	Connect to internal ingredients inventory (if there is one)	Use utility and usability models to improve design and identify future products
	Connect to grocery store data service to get the price and inventory of each ingredient	Number of times the pan is used and its frequency of use

Connect to utility data service to get energy cost	Recipe popularity
Track the amount of time the recipe is being interacted with (cook's total time spent)	Recipe usage
Connect to one or more online shopping apps to order ingredients	
Connect to grocery store service to order ingredients	
Connect to online kitchen scale and other connected kitchen appliances	
Connect to other Internet cookware	
Connect to Internet gadgets	
Connect to housecleaning service	
Interface with platform (general, home, or smart kitchen) of choice	
Focus recipes on non-thermometer-friendly dishes	
Collect demographic info	
Remote access	
Include diagnostic mode	
Get consent to use customer data	
Black box–like functionality	

CHAPTER 10

GETTING STARTED

It started out as just me, but in 18 months GameWare would grow to become 40 percent of Wavefront's revenue, lifting us over the $20 million annual revenue mark, the threshold we needed to go public on the Nasdaq. Which we did.

I wasn't even a gamer. Years before, I liked to play arcade games like Defender and Frogger with friends. And sure, I became addicted to Tron, going on to get the highest score at my university's arcade. But I never lived and breathed video games like some people I knew. That said, when our salesforce started reporting back that one of our main competitors, Alias Research, was experiencing some success in a new market, I put up my hand, asking my boss for some time to look into this electronic gaming thing a little closer.

Now, Andy Smith, our sys admin? He was a gamer. He could rattle off all the moves from all the games. He had a Sega Genesis at home, and he even wore his Sonic the Hedgehog T-shirt to work. He was hard-core. Me? I was fascinated with the opportunity to learn something cool, the opportunity to impact our business, and, if I'm being honest, the opportunity to prove myself as a freshly minted product manager. I may not have been a hard-core gamer, but I knew how to get started. With research—hard-core research that would consume me. This included understanding the customer (game designer and producer) and the market (how games were created and financed and the business models involved) and determining how to modify our technology and business model to make them valuable to the customer. From there I developed our go-to-market strategy and product requirements that I put in front of our prospects for feedback.

However you got here, you're in that same place I was back then: in research mode. In this case, you're putting together your thoughts on how to best approach this IoT thing. That's the purpose of this book, and this chapter is going to describe the approach I used all those years ago, and the same approach I use today with my IoT clients starting to develop their products.

PLANNING

For those people who put up their hands for IoT, the next step after research is planning. A well-written business plan forces you to look in every nook and cranny and every corner case. It establishes your priorities and allows you to measure your progress. It helps identify strategic partners and attract employees—internally and externally. And it flushes out your financing needs and helps you raise these funds if necessary. Part Two, and indeed, this entire book, is designed to help you think through the issues to develop your IoT business plan and requirements document.

Go into the preproduction place knowing things will change. Have the mindset that the IoT business plan and the requirements document are living documents that will be shaped by many customer interactions. Before your product provides you that

24-hour-a-day, 7-day-a-week window into your customer's business, you need to kick things off old school by hitting the road and visiting customers at each major stage of preproduction.

Design-Sell-Build

To get to the starting line, your IoT business plan and requirements doc will be short and initially combined in a 6- to 10-page document. This plan and doc will include the paper version of the product you're going to sell. I subscribe to the Frank Robinson product validation methodology. In fact, I've practiced it since the beginning of my career, when I was pulled out of software development and put into product management to lead the product validation process for our next-generation industrial design software, which incidentally was never built. On the basis of customer feedback, we killed the product before spending any material engineering resources. The knowledge I gained solidified my career as a product manager when I took what I learned and hit the road again using product validation to define the GameWare product line. I've used product validation ever since, now working with my clients to apply the process to their IoT businesses.

For IoT product development, instead of design-build-sell, we *design-sell-build*. This is the ethos of the product validation methodology. Product validation is important because we are so early in this tech evolution that neither the buyer nor the seller knows exactly what's finally required of IoT. Every IoT project I've been directly or indirectly involved with has changed from its inception. And we are not talking nuances. Each project has pivoted between 90 and 180 degrees! I can state with certainty that if your IoT product hasn't taken a major turn before its release, it will take a major turn after its release, so it's better to start selling early.

The stories in this book about my meetings with Pat Dronski in his trailer office on Staten Island, with Paul Brass in his chic high-rise office in Lower Manhattan, and with the cookie factory general, Eric Soderlund, in a borrowed boardroom all happened during product validation. These meetings were part of the first product validation trip we took during the development of ACME Pest's new IoT mousetrap. Once your IoT business plan and requirements doc are written, like us, you must validate your team's thoughts with your target market. This happens before any software or hardware has been developed. Information gathered from these customer visits is used to update the living plan and requirements doc. This is an interactive cycle to be revisited at each and every development milestone during preproduction: concept–ideation–proof of concept–prototype/pilot–minimum viable product (see Figure 10.1).

This book is to guide you to write the first pass of your IoT plan. Plan 1.0 captures the business strategy and product requirements during the internal stages of concept and ideation. After ideation, the plan and requirements doc are packaged into a validation deck and presented to all important stakeholders, especially prospects and customers. This will compel changes, maybe even a pivot, resulting in Plan 2.0. After developing the proof of concept, driven by Plan 2.0, everything is packaged and again presented to your target market. Plan 3.0 supports your customer-infused thinking as you move into the prototype stage (or pilot). By the time you get to your minimum viable product, Plan 4.0 will have radically changed and will continue to change until you move into

Figure 10.1	**Preproduction development cycle**

Plan 1.0		2.0	3.0	4.0		5.0
Preproduction					Production	
Concept	Ideation	POC	Prototype	MVP		

production. Version 5.0 of your IoT business plan and requirements document is your go-to-market plan (see Figure 10.2).

| Figure 10.2 | **Product validation cycle** |

MINIMAL VIABLE PRODUCT (MVP)
CUSTOMER INTERACTION
PROTOTYPE
CUSTOMER INTERACTION
PROOF OF CONCEPT
CUSTOMER INTERACTION
IDEATION
GREEN LIGHT
CONCEPT

STARTING DEVELOPMENT

Ahh, we finally get to talk tech again! Once we have completed the five-step process to create our initial requirements doc (see Chapter 9) and then put the requirements through a couple of cycles of product validation with our prospects, we can go back to the technology and explore what our options are for our prototype.

In-House or Out-of-House

Once we have prioritized our requirements, we need to decide how we are going to develop them. This is the time to take an honest inventory of internal talent to decide which requirements can be developed in-house versus which requirements need to be developed out-of-house. Out-of-house in IoT generally means you're going to a system integrator not only to develop the connecting software but, in some cases, to develop some of the functionality. Or for a discrete product, you may go to a specialized design house that has the expertise you're missing. When done properly and for the right reasons, outsourcing makes sense to fill the skill gaps within your company.

However, all development should be done in-house if possible, with the enterprise going outside only if you need resources before you can hire them. Even then, it may be better to wait. If your invention goes beyond the current state of the art in IoT technology, going out-of-house only buys you bodies, not knowledge. New concepts and approaches will need to be learned by whoever is doing the development, so it's better to make that investment in your own people rather than someone else's.

Build or Buy

This brings us to the build-or-buy decision: which requirements are developed versus which requirements are bought or leased? The high-level answer is, your company must develop the requirements related to the core competencies of its business. When it comes to IoT, these core competencies will be codified by the:

- **Model.** The model quantifies the IoT value proposition and is used by the application and analytics.

- **Application.** This is the distributed software that makes up the front end and back end of your product, orchestrates data flow, and, most importantly, executes the unique functionality of your product.

- **Analytics.** Analytics uses off-the-shelf software with custom recipes to create, modify, and interrogate the model.

For IoT, the rest of the tech can be open-sourced or purchased or leased—there's no reason to reinvent the wheel if wheel making isn't a core competency of your company.

Intellectual Property Strategy

Strategies regarding in-house or out-of-house and build or buy are also guided by your company's intellectual property strategy, and in this case, the intellectual property I'm referring to is mostly the know-how of developing the functionality related to your company's core competencies as they relate to your IoT product. This intellectual property must be developed in-house or developed initially out-of-house with a path to bring the knowledge back in. Again, this intellectual property is for the same trio of value we've been discussing throughout the book: all code, methods, and recipes involved in developing the model, the application, and the analytics of your IoT product.

> **TECH TALK**
>
> To see the competitive importance of patents, see Chapter 6.

Development Order and Dependencies

Once we have the IoT requirements doc 2.0, we're ready to start making development decisions, but how you parse the requirements list, and in what order, is as important as the list itself.

Value in IoT is created top down (see Figure 10.3). At the top of the technology heap is the value proposition, which embodies the value and is quantified during value modeling. This defines

Figure 10.3	**Top-down approach**

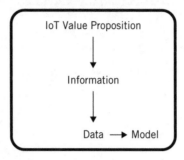

the information needed, which identifies the data in the model that must be collected and transformed. In fact, the purpose of all IoT tech is either to collect data or to transform them into useful information. This brings us to the IoT tech dependency graph (see Figure 10.4).

When looking from a value perspective, the IoT tech dependency graph illustrates dependencies between the tech used in every IoT product. Solid items are tech product classes, and the arrows point in the direction of the dependency.

For example, the model has no dependencies; it is not dependent on any technology. The media protocol, however, is dependent on the radio we choose, but the radio we choose is not dependent on any tech. All the technology referred to in this graph is explained in detail in Part Three, and note, the graph is not intended to show data flow.

Referring to the diagram, the information we need drives the model, which defines the data we need to collect [and our application and analytics package(s)], and those data drive the sensors we need and the external systems we need to interface with. Similarly, the application drives our choice of the development-modeling environment. And analytics drives the technical choices of the

Figure 10.4 | IoT tech dependency graph

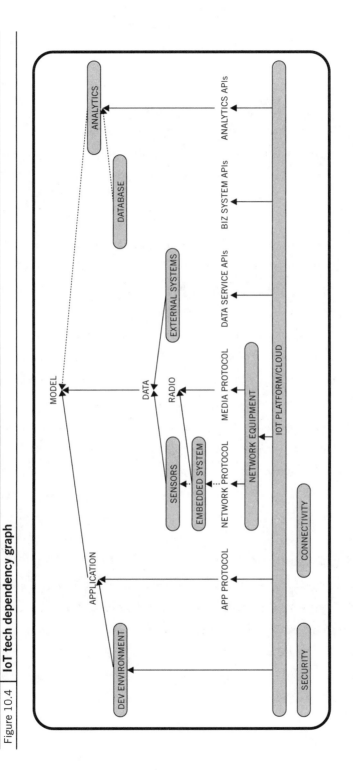

types of analytics packages we require, which in turn drive our choice of the database.

In the end, the IoT platform we choose must support almost everything. I have seen companies make their network or platform decision first. This is wrong. In using the top-down approach, it is almost the last technical choice you make.

Let's use the embedded system as another example. When choosing an embedded system in IoT, an evaluation of the graph shows that this purchasing decision depends on the radio and sensors that the system needs to support. And the sensors depend on the data that need to be collected, which are defined by the model. Looking the other way, the network protocol may be (dotted) dependent on the embedded system chosen. Before shopping for your embedded system, you need to define your model to know what data must be captured. These data dictate the type of sensors to buy and the external systems to connect to. The product's use case dictates the radio type to use. Only after you have made these decisions are you ready to start shopping for an embedded system, selecting it from a narrowed list of qualified competing products that satisfy your sensor and radio needs. Only then is this list further narrowed by other embedded system features such as processing speed and amount of memory.

Buying IoT Technology

The dependency graph is value driven. It's useful for developers, but its purpose is to guide managers in the order of their technology purchases. Actual companies and their product names are not covered because they will change. For an up-to-date list of commercial products, search for the *Iot-Inc Buyer's Guide*, or go to http://www.iot-inc.com/buyers-guide/.

BEST PRACTICES

There is no best way to start your IoT business. Different situations will dictate different paths. Start-ups will have different constraints than will a line of business within large corporations; however, there are best practices for starting your IoT business that have been learned the hard way, by the IoT pioneers.

Start Small but Think Big

Starting small is important for many reasons, some logical and some human. Whether your organization is a start-up or not, your IoT business must start up as one. Vision can't be by consensus. Too many cooks in the kitchen will only serve up blandness. Speed is of paramount importance because the business is going to have to pivot—at least once, but probably more. IoT initiatives represents change. In a larger organization, and when I say larger I mean one with more than 10 employees, change causes anxiety and resistance. Although transparency is key, a smaller team invokes less paranoia than a larger one.

One of the most important messages in this book is to think top down when planning your IoT business. This clarifies and focuses the many moving parts. Top-down thinking is big thinking; it's strategic thinking. More often than not, it is the bling or the shiny things in the lab that set the direction of IoT within the enterprise. That's the wrong approach. That's the tail wagging the dog. Put the time in up front to plan out your IoT business from a value perspective before hard-coding it. You may not be capable of implementing everything at once, nor may it be wise to do so, but do consider how you will create value from the start.

For example, you may not have the in-house data science talent or be able to convince your boss or client of the value of analytics at first. That's fine. In fact, it's the norm. It's difficult for the uninitiated to get their heads around an analytics program, let alone start spending money on it. But it's extremely important to plan for analytics before developing your product because it has direct implications for value. It dictates the information you need and the data you must collect, or more accurately, be able to collect in the future. This has implications for the sensors chosen, the protocols used, and the type of database needed to support things. If analytics is not considered from the start, it will be next to impossible to effectively retrofit the software, let alone the hardware, down the road.

Incubation

Isolate the "start-up" team from the rest of the organization during the preproduction phase of product development. During this period, which is typically under 12 months, it's important that the team isn't under the same quarterly sales pressure as the rest of the organization. This is a strategic investment that must be insulated. At the same time, costs are managed by starting with a small team that only grows as the project requires. Only after the minimum viable product has been developed and vetted by customers can the start-up within the large organization grow into a business unit, line of business, or division with its own P&L or be folded into an existing organizational structure. If it's a smaller organization, the start-up is absorbed into operations and marks the beginning of the company's transformation into an IoT company. Or if it's really small, it becomes the company. The point is that the new IoT organization must be insulated and given the chance to breathe and walk on its own before being absorbed or transformed into something else.

Lean

If you are going to organize as a start-up, it's important that you operate as a start-up, a lean start-up. This means being fast. Put your product in front of prospects as soon as possible, knowing up front it is going to change. You don't want to invest too much into what you are doing until you have proved it. Be data driven. You may believe with all your heart that you have conceived of the perfect product, but let the prospect decide that. Test, measure, and refine using the *design-sell-build* validation methodology. Continually learn from customers at each step of the preproduction development cycle. Be flexible; be able and willing to pivot away from the original vision to a new reality, one that will make you money.

If you're going to operate as a start-up, it's important you grow as a start-up. Start with a founder, a tech lead, and maybe a sales and marketing lead and grow from there. Add headcount only as necessary. During preproduction the technical team will grow as development ramps up and new skill sets like data science are added. As you get closer to the minimum viable product, sales, marketing, manufacturing, and support will need to grow as the business shifts from preproduction to production and commercialization.

I have seen this start-up structure work best, but I've also seen other organizational structures used in larger companies. A center of excellence, consisting of internal and external IoT experts, can be used to guide a larger team, and so too can a cross-business steering committee made up of internal employees. However, I believe in order to have the responsiveness necessary, decision making needs to be more local, as does accountability. If the talent is available, a center of excellence or steering committee is best utilized as an advisory board to the small (internal) start-up.

Budgeting

Funding the development of an IoT product is different than for traditional products. This is simply because it's new. The tech is new, and the business is new; and as such it will take longer and need more resources to launch a product. I recommend breaking down the budget into preproduction, production, and launch. For most traditional companies, preproduction has the most risk and is underfunded, mostly because of the lack of experience. Therefore, you need to further break preproduction down into budgetary buckets that correspond with the development milestones of concept, ideation, proof of concept, prototype, and minimum viable product. And part of the preproduction budget must go to product validation, described earlier, that is, to design-sell-build, to ensure the product is commercially viable.

Education

Although you want to operate your start-up separately from the rest of the organization, it needs to be part of the larger organization. Transparency is key to dampen any internal forces that may hamper progress. One of the best ways to do this is through education, or as some may call it, evangelism. Manage up and manage down by educating up and educating down. As the budget and resources grow, there will be more scrutiny from people in management. Educate them more. Inform leadership on your progress and the organizational changes required to support the product once launched. This book is a great resource for that—evangelize others in the company about the topics covered in here.

Transparency reduces anxiety and threats. Your internal start-up will need the rest of the organization's support if it is to become successful. Upcoming organizational changes can't be a surprise or they will face resistance and backlash. Hold regular brown-bag lunches or whatever vehicle your company uses for informal education.

While educating up and down, you must be educating yourself and the rest of the start-up team members. You and your start-up team must be *the* IoT experts of your company. This means identifying knowledge gaps and then leveraging online resources like http://www.iot-inc.com, as well as attending IoT conferences and online training like http://www.brucesinclair.net/online-training/. I recommended joining an IoT meetup if you have one in your area and the appropriate IoT consortium, alliance, or group. You can also get involved in standards organizations with a degree of involvement commensurate with the resources available (see Figure 10.5). Very large organizations should have multiple employees dedicated full time, while smaller entities may only be able to send one representative to attend quarterly meetings to get informed and to make contacts.

Figure 10.5	**IoT industry groups**

Consortia	**Standards Bodies**
• Industrial Internet Consortium	• IETF
• Open Connectivity Foundation	• IEEE
• Thread Group	
• LoRa Alliance	
• IPSO Alliance	
• OpenFog Consortium	

This chapter outlines how I have started with my IoT clients. The ideas here have been learned the hard way, by the pioneers, so consider following their path instead of completely finding a new one.

• • •

Next up is Part Three, where we get into the tech, down and deep; at least deep enough for managers to have a meaningful discussions with the technical folks.

PART THREE

A TECH DEEP DIVE INTO IOT

In this section, we dive deeper into the technology and break it down into its four main components: the software-defined product, the hardware-defined product, the network fabric, and the external systems. We then break them down further, along with analytics and cybersecurity, to a level deep enough to understand the tech yet not deep enough to code it. The Internet of Things by nature is very technical, so to effectively use it, it is vital to understand it. I believe you need to understand how it works before you can put it to work.

Before diving in, I recommend you read or reread Chapter 1, "IoT Tech Defined from a Value Perspective." Chapter 1 provides an overview of the tech and how its different components work together.

THE SOFTWARE-DEFINED PRODUCT

OVERVIEW

From a business perspective, there's no technology more important. The software-defined product (SDP), sometimes called the digital twin, is what enables value creation in the Internet of Things. It is the virtual representation of the product's IoT functionality. It is this digitization of the physical into the digital that enables the IoT product to interface with the Internet like any other Internet software. That's the source of its power. The IoT product is software (see Figure 11.1).

The SDP is separated into two parts: the cybermodel and the application (see Figure 11.2). The cybermodel encodes the product's value, and the application executes the model to create value. It's important to separate the two because analytics also uses the model. Analytics builds the model and interrogates it to create value. This again is the trio of value creation in IoT: the model, application, and analytics.

Consider the IoT mousetrap. This model does not represent what it looks like or its physical structure; instead it represents how it works, the environment it's in, and the migration patterns

| Figure 11.1 | The software-defined product within the IoT product |

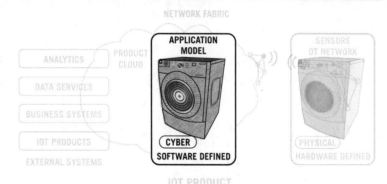

of mice. The model is a simulation of how the IoT mousetrap catches mice. Its analytics incorporates real-world data to improve the simulation, and its application executes the simulation to give it its functionality, making the physical product better . . . making a better mousetrap.

CYBERMODEL

Modeling is not new. I started my career building models to describe the shape of objects, how they moved and how they looked. In my first professional job before I modeled dinosaurs, I worked in the craniofacial research lab at my university, using MRI scans to create 3D models of the human skull and its muscles. Since then I've worked on models from the video game and military simulation industries.

Fast-forward a couple of decades: I was recently advising an IoT client, an aerospace company, when one of the engineers in the room pointed out that he and his coworkers had been modeling for years. Which is true. Just as I had done in computer animation, they had modeled physical function. CAD employs

| Figure 11.2 | The software-defined product |

functional models such as those used in finite element analysis to describe energy transfer. In both computer animation and CAD, we model the physical or physics' representation of the world—what it looks like, how it moves, and how it works.

What's different is that in IoT there is a closed feedback loop that continuously senses the world, producing data to improve the simulation and how we interact with it.

Types of Cybermodels

At a high level, there are two types of models: the parametric model and the stochastic model. The parametric model is your more classical mathematics or physics model—an equation of a spring, for example. But it turns out that representing a spring with the simple mathematical relationship $F = kX$ does not even come close to describing what happens in the real world because it does not take into account enough real-world variables.

Stochastic models are different; they are statistically driven. An analogy I like to use is sometimes found in action movies. The protagonist has a grainy, unrecognizable photo of the villain. Over time with the help of a powerful supercomputer and a crack team of analysts, the face image becomes clearer and more recognizable. It starts out abstract, but over time it gets progressively clearer until the villain is finally recognized and the manhunt begins in earnest.

I like to think of cybermodels in that way because it's how they work—start off with a general representation and then refine the model over time to make it more accurate. The more data points collected, the more accurate the model. Think about how this looks in two dimensions: when you only have 3 points, everything looks like a triangle; with 8 points, there's more fidelity; and after 1,000 points, the shape forms. Think about the mathematics behind cybermodels in the same way.

Example

Let's look at that simple spring again. We have traditionally described the spring with physics (see Figure 11.3). $F = kX$ mathematically maps compression and elongation—the spring is either squished together or pulled apart, depending on whether the force is negative or positive.

This equation works great to explain the concept in high school textbooks, but in the real world, if you want to know how far a spring will compress or expand due to a known force, the beloved spring equation is far too simplistic to give you an accurate causal relationship between force and length change. Many more variables need to be taken into account. They include the type of metal of the spring, its shape, its temperature, the viscosity of the environment

| Figure 11.3 | **Different models to represent the simple spring** |

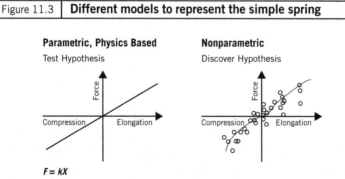

it's in, etc. In this example, even in the case of the simplest of parts, it is more accurate to employ a stochastic statistics model.

The stochastic model is created by measuring the cause and effect of the variable(s) to be measured in your model. In this case, we apply force 1 and measure compression 1, force 2 and compression 2, and so on. From those data points, a higher-order representation is created.

The more data points, the more accurate the model. For that particular spring, we want to get to the point that when you apply a force in the real world, you can estimate its compression by executing its model in the virtual world.

As Used in IoT

It's important to note that the IoT product is never represented with just a single cybermodel. There will be different models for each of its IoT functions, each with their own simulations to be run. A single IoT product can have tens, hundreds, even thousands of different models, each with its own purpose. These models are shaped and used offline by analytics and used online by the application during product operation.

Once we can describe the model mathematically, the application can then look at it from different points of view and solve it in different ways, drawing out different information that contributes to its value. But it always starts as a statistical sampling of cause and effect. Understanding the stochastic model is fundamental to understanding the models used in analytics.

APPLICATION

The application defines what the product does—its functionality. This is where the majority of software development occurs. The application acts upon the model or executes the model to produce the intended value.

It orchestrates data flow, pulling data from sensors in or on the product and from external systems on the Internet. It interfaces with the analytics, feeding it data and using its insights to improve product operation. And it interfaces with people, both the users of the product and the customers who work on its back end.

The application, like the model and analytics, can be distributed over all computing surfaces: embedded systems, routers and switches in the IT network, gateways in the OT network, servers in the cloud, the desktop computer and mobile device. Its location or locations depend on the required functionality and use case.

THE IOT DRYER

My clothes dryer at home is really simple. It has a timer and start button and a couple of ways to dial in how I want the clothes dried. Sometimes my clothes are too dry and wrinkly, and sometimes they're not dry enough, but generally the results are good enough. How do we use the Internet of Things to add value to this 75-year-old technology? The knee-jerk reaction is to connect it to our mobile phone to command it, to control it.

> **TECH TALK**
>
> For more information on value modeling, see Chapter 2.

But as discussed in Chapter 2, a connected product is generally not good enough, or better stated, its incremental value does not justify its incremental cost. Instead of creating a connected dryer, let's instead create an IoT dryer.

The first step is to define the incremental value of our IoT dryer. In this case our IoT value proposition is *to dry clothes as quickly as possible or as cheaply as possible while maintaining their integrity*— that is, so they don't shrink, stretch, or wrinkle. We have now qualified the value of the dryer; next we must quantify it with a model.

To build our cybermodel, we look to the science of evaporation, because effectively what we are trying to do is change the state of water in the clothes from liquid into gas.

Evaporation depends on heat and ventilation. And it turns out that ventilation, the sweeping of H_2O molecules off the boundary layer of the clothes, is more effective than heat, which excites the molecules to the point where they reach another energy state and jump off the clothes. The IoT dryer will balance ventilation and heat based on the characteristics of the load, for speed or cost.

Cybermodel

This cybermodel is a function of ventilation, temperature, clothes weight, and energy pricing.

$$\text{Time/energy} = f(\text{ventilation, temperature, clothes weight, energy pricing}).$$

Those are the four macro variables that we need to understand and further break down in order to quantify the value proposition.

The dryer is a pretty simple device. It is ventilated by the fan at the back and by the clothes being tossed around by the rotating drum. Temperature is controlled by the heating element in front of the fan. The best drying, it turns out, occurs when the temperature of the clothes is the same temperature as the air. If the temperature of the air becomes higher than the temperature of the clothes, the hotter air causes the clothes to burn. If the temperature of the air is less than the temperature of the clothes, the cooler air causes the clothes to wrinkle.

For ventilation, we need to capture the speed of the fan and the angular velocity of the drum, both of which are related to air flow. This leads to:

Ventilation = f(fan speed, angular velocity)

For temperature, we need to measure air temperature derived from the temperature of the heating element, and we also need to measure the temperature of the clothes. This leads to:

Temperature = f(heating element temp, clothes temp)

And finally, we need to measure the weight of the clothes and the cost of energy at the time of drying. Expanding our value model, we get:

Time/energy = f(fan speed, angular velocity of drum, heating element temp, clothes temp, load weight, energy pricing)

These variables are the data we need for our cybermodel. Our engineers can find the right sensors to capture the data and the right data services from the utility company to provide up-to-date energy pricing.

Our model is built over time, by the data coming in from our sensors and the Internet. Our job as managers is not to further develop the model; that's the job of engineers. Our modeling job, the job of value creation, is finished after we define its variables—in this case, fan speed, angular velocity of drum, heating element temp, clothes temp, clothes weight, and energy pricing (see Figure 11.4).

Application

The application interrogates the model and actuates the hardware-defined product in real time. It samples data from the sensors and

Figure 11.4	Value modeling for the IoT dryer

Dry clothes as quickly as possible or for as cheaply as possible while maintaining their integrity

Model
- Time/energy = f(ventilation, heat, pricing)
- Time/energy = f(fan speed, angular velocity, load weight, heater temperature, drum temperature, energy pricing)

Application
- Interrogates model and actuates hardware-defined product

Analytics
- Build models linking pivot variables to outcomes
- Use descriptive analytics to report on cost savings
- Use predictive analytics to estimate when clothes will be dried and when rollers will wear out

data services and executes the local drying model. Since the model is an equation, we can manipulate it, rearrange it, and solve it to meet our different end goals (speed, cost). We then use the variables of the solved model to actuate the temperature of the heating coil, the angular velocity of the drum, and the speed of the fan. In effect, we are changing the dryer's microsettings to dry the clothes either as fast as possible or for as little cost as possible, for that particular load and energy cost.

Since this is done in real time, software will be running locally in the dryer's embedded system actuating its hardware in accordance with the dryer's cybermodels.

Computing is also happening in the cloud; this is after all an IoT product. Besides the back-office management system to be used for maintenance and support, model management is also the responsibility of the application—updating the code in the embedded system through an over-the-air (OTA) mechanism, as it's improved over time. This same OTA mechanism is used by the application to update security and to add new functionality to the IoT dryer as it's developed.

Therefore, connectivity to the Internet is needed to get electricity pricing updates; perform maintenance if necessary; update the model, application, and security; and remotely start and stop the dryer. Building and refining the cybermodel are also done in the cloud.

The Analytics

Analytics is all about creating a great model and then comparing that model with the data collected to make decisions.

As mentioned in the earlier spring example, the statistical model's accuracy, and therefore value, increases with the number of data points used in its creation. And data points will come not only from this single IoT dryer, but from all of these dryers sold. The IoT dryer's model will improve over time and will be updated within the product by the back-end model management software.

Streaming analytics is used to control the dryer in the present. Descriptive analytics is used to understand what happened in the past by creating a report on how, for example, you use your dryer and the costs incurred. And predictive analytics is used to predict what will happen in the future—for example, to estimate how long it will take to dry the load or to estimate when a part is going to break.

Now, after all that, is the IoT dryer more valuable than the connected dryer? Sure. Is its incremental value worth its incremental cost? That depends on the customer, but this was at least a good example of how the software-defined product would be used to improve a product we use all the time.

• • •

This concept of virtualizing the essence of the product into software is key to value creation, but we still need to operate in the physical world, so the next chapter covers the hardware-defined product.

CHAPTER 12

THE HARDWARE-DEFINED PRODUCT

Let's talk hardware now. For our purposes, the hardware-defined product consists of the hardware required to capture, process, and transmit data at the edge (see Figure 12.1). This comprises the embedded system and the sensors and actuators (see Figure 12.2).

EMBEDDED SYSTEMS

An embedded system consists of an MPU (microprocessing unit), an I/O front end, power, and sometimes basic sensors and radios (from Bluetooth to LPWA). An MPU, unlike a CPI (central processing unit) used in a Linux-based gateway, uses internal rather than external memory. This constrains the available storage.

The MPU runs a real-time operating system (often referred to as an RTOS) that stores and executes local applications, manages communications with sensors on the OT (operational technology) network, and runs local security and analytics.

Each embedded system comes with either an SDK (software development kit) or an API (application programming inter-

Figure 12.1	The hardware-defined product within the IoT product

face) or both. Choosing an embedded system means choosing a development environment. This development environment supports different programming languages and networking protocols through its networking stack. Therefore, you need to ensure that the embedded system you choose is compatible with or can be made compatible with both your application development environment and the protocols you need to support. Therefore, choosing an embedded system is driven by your requirements document and development environment.

The order of the technology chosen has a top-down hierarchy. We first ask, which sensors are able to capture the data we need? Next, which interfaces are used by the sensors we need? And when I say interfaces, I refer to protocols (media, networking, and application) and APIs, both of which have implications for your development environment.

So for the hardware-defined product and OT networking tech, the embedded system is the last thing you choose. On one hand, it is chosen to support the sensor, which supports the data, which support the information, which supports the value. On the other hand, it must support the application protocol, which supports the application, which supports the information, which sup-

Figure 12.2 | **The hardware-defined product**

ports the value. See Chapter 10 for a complete description of IoT technical dependencies.

SENSORS AND ACTUATORS

A sensor's transducer transforms one energy form into another (see Figure 12.3). And the second energy form is generally direct current, often between 5 and −5 volts. Within sensors, this direct current is converted with an A/D converter into a digital value—the payload to be transported for processing. Actuator communication goes in the opposite direction—a digital signal from the application is converted into an analog signal that powers some effect in the physical world.

The good news is that there will be a sensor that matches your needs. Sensors have been big business for over 50 years, so there are literally over a million SKUs (choices) to choose from (see

Figure 12.3 | **The sensor**

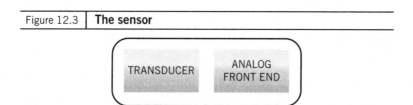

Figure 12.4	Sensor types

- Acceleration/Vibration
- Acoustic/Ultrasonic
- Chemical/Gas
- Electric/Magnetic Flow
- Force/Load/Torque/Strain
- Humidity/Moisture
- Leak/Level
- Optical
- Motion/Velocity/Displacement
- Position/Presence/Proximity
- Pressure
- Temperature

Figure 12.4). What is a challenge is finding the right one. The sensor type will be defined by the data requirements, but other kinds of functionality that must be considered too are the power profile (how electricity and how much electricity is being used), fidelity (accuracy), noise (random errors), and manageability. But even when the sensors look good on paper, they must be tested, because they don't always operate as advertised. Sometimes their behavior is counterintuitive. For example, the highest-fidelity sensor is not necessarily the best sensor because of false negatives that must be filtered by the application. Sensors, therefore, should be benchmarked for your individual needs.

The sensor and the connected sensor are two very different things. To help connect it, the sensor needs an embedded system, radio, and power (see Figure 12.5).

There are two different types of connected sensors: embedded sensors and stand-alone sensors.

Embedded and Stand-Alone Sensors

When sensors are embedded directly within the product during design, we call it a greenfield installation. An example is the

Figure 12.5	The connected sensor/actuator

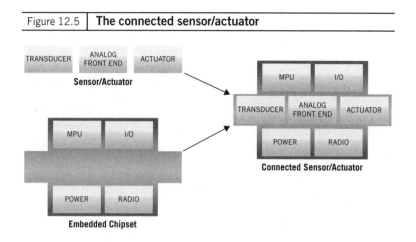

embedded sensors found within an IoT clothes dryer. In these installations, one or more sensors are controlled by a single embedded chipset.

In brownfield installations, existing products, systems, or environments are retrofitted with connected sensors. Expensive equipment with a life cycle of 10, 15, even 25 years will not be replaced, so to instrument them, an exoskeleton sensor network is fastened on top of the equipment, leaving existing communications alone (see Figure 12.6).

Device Management

Device management, or more accurately, connected sensor management, will be an ongoing activity, so it should be considered in advance of any purchase decision. Device management consists of provisioning, configuration, and maintenance.

Provisioning is the process of making the connection between the sensor and the embedded system on the OT network, and the application on the IT network. Authentication of the sensors, as part of security, is part of provisioning. Configuration is the process of associating metadata with the sensor to provide contextual information. These metadata are associated with the data

Figure 12.6 | **Different types of connected sensors**

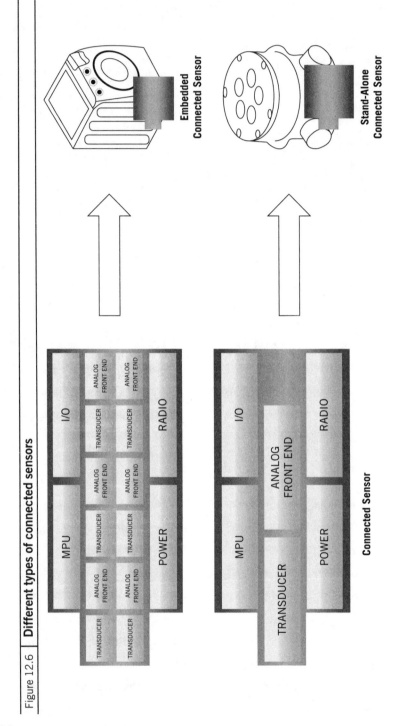

payload (e.g., what the data are, units of the data, location of the device, . . .) and the software and hardware that captured the data (e.g., device ID, firmware version, security version, software version, . . .). Maintenance is the process of changing the software in the embedded system that manages the sensor or multiple sensors. This is used to fix bugs, to update end node security, and, if necessary, to extend the metadata structure.

In greenfield installations, the provisioning and configuration are done as part of product design and then "manufactured" along with the product. And testing is part of product testing. The maintenance system must be designed into the product, but it lives independently in the form of an OTA subsystem to update the embedded firmware or software.

In brownfield deployments, there are other considerations. Provisioning and configuration are done "manually" for each instance of the product. The questions to ask are: How manual is the process? Are there tools, such as mobile phone apps, that can be used in the field, or is the process more complicated? How is testing done? And what is the mechanism used to physically install the stand-alone sensors? Take time to understand your choices, because the answers to these questions have big implications on human resource costs. Once the device is provisioned and configured, future maintenance is done the same way as in the greenfields, with an automated OTA system.

Sensor Pricing

The good news is that the price of sensors has dropped. In the last 15 years, prices have decreased from an average of $22 to $1 due to the proliferation of the phones we carry in our pockets. Mobile phones are big sensor arrays, and the sheer volume of the phones keeps forcing the prices further and further down. Of course, this is only for a subset of sensor classes, but the needed efficiencies in manufacturing have had a halo effect on all sensors.

• • •

This chapter covered what's living on the OT network but not the network itself. The next chapter examines the entire network fabric, including the OT network.

THE NETWORK FABRIC

NETWORK OVERVIEW

In this chapter, we are going to discuss what can be literally described as the Internet of Things—the network fabric connecting the major parts of the IoT product together (see Figure 13.1).

Following the sensor data, we start in the operational technology (OT) network, cross to the information technology (IT) network, more often than not with a radio, and then continue to a local cloud (on prem) or directly to the backhaul that connects the local network to the Internet and product cloud.

The IoT platform is a key product category. It consists of software that interfaces with the product cloud and varying amounts of the IT network and possibly the OT network. A major benefit is that the platform is packaged and integrated, sometimes with a dev environment that yields shorter development times and better security.

I don't want to minimize the importance of the network fabric, but when looked at from a value perspective, it's the plumbing that facilitates value creation. Although there are exceptions, it is not an area of intellectual property that the company needs

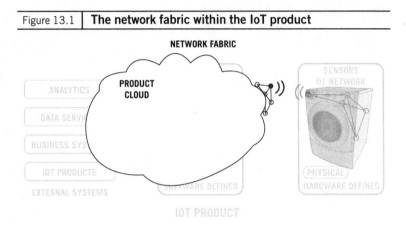

Figure 13.1 | The network fabric within the IoT product

to bring in-house. Although important to understand, it is not important to own or build from scratch, and it will be the IoT tech that's commoditized first.

COMMUNICATION STANDARDIZATION AND PROTOCOLS

Although a little dry, *protocols* (a term I'll use interchangeably with *layers* and *standards*) are the basis of network communication and standardization in the Internet of Things. The lack of standardization, along with monetization challenges and security concerns, is slowing the adoption of IoT.

Until now, IoT has grown in industry as independent silos—independent silos that lacked standardization because the protocols did not need to talk to each other. They were not the Internet of Things; they were just things. If sophisticated, they were the local network of things (M2M), but more likely they were only connected to displays (also a form of M2M) that were connected overall with the "Sneakernet" of Things.

Nested Layers

In computer networking, protocols are organized as a stack, so the first thing to understand is that there is not a single network protocol in the Internet of Things; there are three network protocols and an upcoming fourth. There are protocols for the radio, for how we move packets around the network, and for how we contextualize the data in a way that makes it consumable by the application. Let's go through each of these layers (see Figure 13.2).

Figure 13.2	Payload and layers

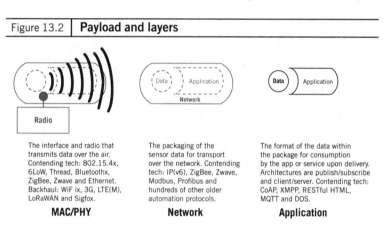

The interface and radio that transmits data over the air. Contending tech: 802.15.4x, 6LoW, Thread, Bluetoothx, ZigBee, Zwave and Ethernet. Backhaul: WiF ix, 3G, LTE(M), LoRaWAN and Sigfox.

MAC/PHY

The packaging of the sensor data for transport over the network. Contending tech: IP(v6), ZigBee, Zwave, Modbus, Profibus and hundreds of other older automation protocols.

Network

The format of the data within the package for consumption by the app or service upon delivery. Architectures are publish/subscribe and client/server. Contending tech: CoAP, XMPP, RESTful HTML, MQTT and DOS.

Application

Media Layer

Let's start with the first layer, the media layer, or what's sometimes referred to as the MAC/PHY layer. This is the only layer that includes hardware. Generally in IoT, it is a radio, but it does not have to be; it can also be hardwired with the Ethernet protocol. The radios we generally deploy in IoT are 802.15.4, used by old-school ZigBee and Zwave, and new-school 6LoPAN, which is part of the even newer school, Thread. Next we have 802.11, which is Wi-Fi, and 802.15.1 which is Bluetooth. There is cellular technology (1G through LTE and now 5G), and more recently there are low-power, wide-area (LPWA) radios in which protocol standardization is still in progress. Radio protocols are not going to consolidate, because each radio has different characteristics. Referring back to your high school physics, remember that the different characteristics come down to wave mechanics.

Different use cases demand different radios—with the major variables being power (how much it uses), frequency (fidelity and bandwidth), and range (how far it reaches). Depending on these radio characteristics, they are used in personal area networks, local area networks, or wide-area networks. In addition to physics, sometimes economics affects radio choice. Some radio technologies such as cellular use a carrier model to provide infrastructure, while others may require the enterprise to deploy and maintain its own infrastructure gateways, antennas, etc.

Personal area networks fit squarely with Bluetooth, although the SIG has muddied the waters with a mesh network initiative. Bluetooth is generally a low-power, high-frequency, short-range radio, which for a lot of close-proximity applications makes a lot of sense. Wi-Fi certainly has enough bandwidth for any IoT application and a mid-distance range, but it consumes a lot of energy. While Bluetooth can use batteries, Wi-Fi must be plugged into the wall.

The 802.15.4 network is often referred to as a lossy network or low-power lossy network. These radios are organized as a mesh network and used in the home, on pipelines, and in other infrastructure IoT deployments. A mesh network is an alternative to routing with less overhead (memory, computation) while withstanding nodes going down, just as in a routed network. But as the name implies, it will generally lose more data after being compromised than its routed counterpart.

I don't recommend ZigBee or Zwave for any new deployments. Despite propaganda that says otherwise, they are the definition of a closed and proprietary silo. Taking over for these old-school protocols is Thread. Thread is also based on 802.15.4 and is designed as a replacement for ZigBee and Zwave, but unlike its predecessors, it's based on the open protocol IPv6 (Internet protocol version 6) via its slimmer self, 6LoPAN.

If you have ac power, Wi-Fi is the protocol of choice on the local area network. It has enough bandwidth for almost any IoT use case, and its ubiquity makes it cost effective. Wi-Fi is generally deployed in closed spaces but has been effectively used with repeaters at larger scale outdoors. A downside can be its relatively complex initial setup.

Cellular, in the flavors of 2G, 3G, 4G, and now LTE-M and NB-IoT, makes sense for remote and moving things that require lots of bandwidth. These star topology networks are very reliable, but they come at a price. Although they have been used in telematics (a form of M2M) for years, the business models must change. Mobile operators realize this and will adapt their monetization strategy or be marginalized and relegated to the fewer and fewer use cases that can afford them and cannot use LPWA. Carriers could have a bright future, but their business needs to expand beyond only cellular and beyond only connectivity to perhaps platforms that include different radios, storage, and billing as well as system integration.

LPWA is the newest radio on the IoT block. As advertised, it requires very little power but can communicate over long distances. Its small payload size and bandwidth, however, limit its use cases. But its relatively low monetary cost expands its world of use cases, making possible IoT products we aren't even dreaming about yet. As with cellular, LPWA takes the form of a star topology (see Figure 13.3), which is better suited for a one-to-one communication model lacking the advantages of mesh networking. The bandwidth is low, and when I say low, I mean bytes-per-minute low, but this does have its advantages. Replacing sensor batteries

| Figure 13.3 | Star topology |

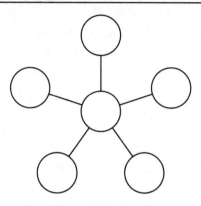

is operationally intensive and costly. LPWA still requires batteries to be changed, but often it's due to their being older than their shelf life rather than because their power was used up. The business model for LPWA networks is broad. You can purchase the network's components and build your own network, as in the cases of 15.4, Wi-Fi, and Bluetooth; on the other hand, a number of LPWA operators are emerging that allow you to subscribe to their networks, as you do for cellular.

Standardization will not reduce the number of media layer protocols. Because of the different use cases they support, we will have at least these five radio classes in IoT's future. From a business perspective, we are not in favor of one radio type over another. Which radio is chosen is dictated by our requirements doc in support of gathering the type of data we need, in order to create the information we need, to support our IoT value proposition.

Network Layer

Next, we move on to the networking layer. Unlike the media layer and the application layer, the network layer is going to be standardized. Today, the network layer spans both the IT and

OT networks of an IoT deployment. It's on the OT side of the house where you'll find over 100 proprietary network protocols: Modbus, Profibus, TLS. . . . Every industry independently developed its own networking protocol, custom-made for its domain, whether it was for the car (CAN bus), for building automation (BACnet), or for the smart grid (OSGP).

On the IT side of the house, we have standardized on IP (Internet protocol). We are currently using IP version 4 (IPv4) and transitioning worldwide to IPv6 that has an address space big enough to give a unique address to every sensor on earth, in fact big enough to give a unique address to every grain of sand on earth.

The extension of IP from the IT network into the OT network is inevitable. There are too many advantages of using one network protocol, from sensor to public cloud, for it not to happen. The immediate benefits include lower cost and better security and not being locked into any particular vendor.

Another name for IP is the integration protocol because everybody knows it, making its deployment relatively simple. With IP you have economy of scale, security benefits, and flexibility, and lastly you have people that just know it.

Application Layer

The last IoT protocol is the application protocol. Application protocols include metadata to go along with the raw data payload. The class of application protocol depends on the architecture of your application. Publish-subscribe protocols that message all nodes include MQTT and XMPP. Client-server protocols that utilize gets and puts include RESTful HTML, CoAP, and DDS.

Application protocols are important because they contextualize the data payload so it can be used efficiently by the application. Going back to our IoT dryer example, let's say our sensors are pulling out 36.2, 1.24, 1506.0, a continuous string of numbers transmitted over the network. But what do they mean? What do they represent?

To answer those questions, we have to understand how these data were saved in our database's memory so we can read the data out of that memory in a sensible way. Requiring a "map" of how the data were stored is very inefficient. Just as the browser has no idea how the data were stored on the server, we must take the same approach with IoT data. We need to store what the data mean along with their values, instead of having to use a lookup table or algorithm after the fact to determine information about the data collected. This is what application protocols do; they put a contextual layer around the data. Instead of reading a string of numbers that require some sort of algorithm to understand what they are, we read 97.16: temperature in degrees Fahrenheit, from sensor B, in dryer serial number X, at time Y; 1.24: angular velocity in rotations per second, from sensor A, in dryer serial number X, at time Y; 1506.0: weight in grams, from sensor C, in dryer serial number X, at time Y.

By using an application protocol, the application can consume the data in a more efficient way, no matter where the data reside.

Meta Layer

A pseudo fourth layer, emerging one by one in different industries, is the metadata layer. That is a map of all legitimate metadata along with their meaning and units. Media protocols allow different radios to talk to each other. Network protocols allow different networks to talk to each other. Application protocols allow different applications to talk to each other . . . as long as they are using the same vocabulary, which is where metadata protocols come in. This really allows applications from different developers, even from different industries, to talk to each other with a common vocabulary, a common understanding of what the metadata represent. Think of an autonomous vehicle talking to a smart city. Although these two IoT products may use the same application protocol enabling us to know that the data value, 6, is velocity, if the car represents velocity in meters per second and the city represents velocity as miles per hour, we still have a contextual and, hence, metadata problem. The respective applications running the vehicle and the city need to reconcile the meaning of speed. Although we are starting to see this within certain industries, e.g., MTConnect for the manufacturing industry, I predict we will see a syntax developed to cross industry silos, like what's needed in the vehicle-city example.

Follow the Data Example

A useful way to think about the relationship between the three IoT protocols, or layers, and the data is to use the analogy of the Russian matryoshka, or nesting, doll. A data value starts inside the application protocol, which is inside the network protocol, which is inside the radio protocol. Each protocol is unpacked at different points along the journey from sensor to application. Let's continue our IoT dryer example, following the journey of data point 97.16 from temperature sensor to application, which stores it in a database on the server for further analysis.

The sensor interprets temperature and converts its output voltage into the digital equivalent of 97.16. This is the data payload—it's what we need to get to the application (see Figure 13.4).

The embedded system's computing wraps the application protocol around the payload and carries with it the units of measurement, the serial number of the dryer, the time the data point was captured, and other information about the contents of the data and the hardware and software that stored the contents (see Figure 13.5).

Figure 13.4	**Payload**

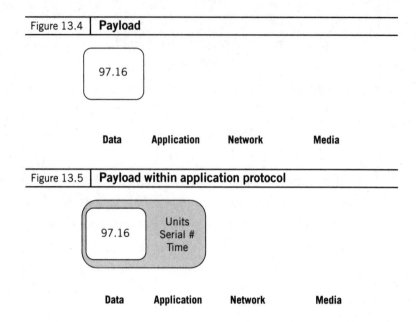

Figure 13.5	**Payload within application protocol**

The application protocol, along with the data it holds, is packed into the OT network protocol and sent along the dryer's internal OT network to the dryer's radio (see Figure 13.6).

Figure 13.6	**Payload within OT network protocol**

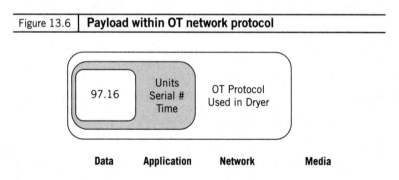

The OT network protocol, containing the application protocol, containing the payload, is then packed into the media protocol, corresponding to the dryer's radio type (in this case, Wi-Fi), and sent through the air from the radio transmitter in the dryer to the radio receiver in a gateway (Wi-Fi router) on the home IT network (see Figure 13.7).

Figure 13.7 | **Payload within media protocol**

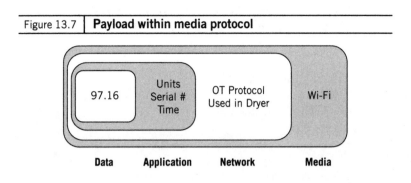

There the radio protocol is stripped off, leaving the OT network protocol. Since the receiver is on an IT network, the gateway must be used to unpack the application protocol and its data from the OT network protocol and then pack it into the IT network protocol, IP. After it is in the Internet protocol format, the application protocol along with its data payload (97.16) is sent along the IT network to the backhaul connection, where it leaves the house, finds some fiber, and makes its way to the Internet (see Figure 13.8).

Figure 13.8 | **Payload within Internet protocol**

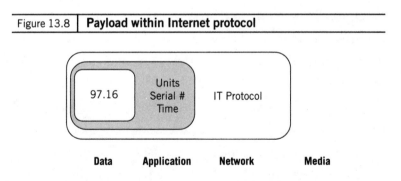

While in the Internet, the packet of data is routed, via IP, to, and is ingested into, the product cloud and then routed to the application server. The OS in the server strips off the network layer and delivers the data, packed in the application protocol, to the application (see Figure 13.9).

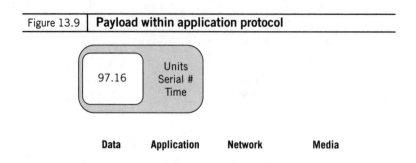

Figure 13.9 | **Payload within application protocol**

The application, running on the server, unpacks the application protocol, ingesting the 97.16 payload along with its metadata so that the application knows what it is. The data are acted upon immediately or are stored in a database on another server along with the metadata for future use by the application or analytics.

The type of application, network, and radio protocols used will be guided by the use case and our requirements, and this is the concern of the engineering team charged with implementation. Often when I first talk to clients, they are already debating, will it be Bluetooth or Wi-Fi, and are already deep into their platform selection. That's wrong; it's the tail wagging the dog. While it's important to understand how it works, the first step is to define value, then the data we need, and only after that do we consider the technology.

Having said that, there is one networking tech that we should be insistent upon, and that's the networking protocol used—it must be the IP. This should be standardized as much as possible. The IT network will of course use IP, but we must demand that the OT network use it as much as reasonably possible. This is not because we think it's technically superior but because it is economically superior as per the earlier attributes of lower cost, greater simplicity, and more security. If your vendor does not offer IP today in its OT network, then you need to change vendors or demand that it's put on their road map. This will help move the needle on standardization and give your company, and the industry as a whole, more and better options in the future.

Let's pop up a layer and get back to the different parts of the network fabric.

OPERATIONAL TECHNOLOGY NETWORK

OT is the technology required to support the operations of the IoT product (system or environment). The purpose of the OT network is to transport data between the sensors or actuators and the IT network that eventually takes the data to the application (see Figure 13.10).

OT networks can be personal area networks, local area networks, or wide-area networks. They can be really small, like what's inside a smart watch; they can be inside a dryer or a building; or they can be really big, spanning a city or even a country.

Since OT networks evolved in isolation within different industry verticals, they almost all use proprietary networking protocols, as we discussed earlier. These proprietary protocols were custom built for specific business operations such as process automation, industrial control, building automation, power system automation, point of sale . . . They were also built for home automation,

Figure 13.10	**The OT network**

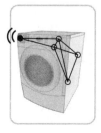

vehicles . . . the list goes on. Along with proprietary protocols come proprietary hardware and vendor lock-in. This has led to the Internet of Gateways—proprietary gateways for proprietary networking protocols and other gateways to convert these proprietary networking protocols to the Internet protocol. Not so good.

OT networks are by nature isolated and can be decades old. To connect a SCADA (supervisory control and data acquisition) system, for example, to the Internet of Things, there are two options: you can tap into the existing network with a gateway and translate the proprietary networks in preparation for the IT network and backhaul, or you can build an overlay IP network—parallel to and independent of the OT network. OT managers and technicians often choose the second option to not risk disrupting the operations of their business, but there can be a loss of some important data by using overlay networks. In some cases, this retrofit may go as far as to duplicate the sensors, completely isolating the two networks.

One of my clients was building an overlay product to instrument midpriced manufacturing machinery that was 10 to 15 years old on average. On one hand, it was a lot easier, technically and politically, to not tap directly into the machine bus and to use our own sensors. But on the other hand, by not going directly to the source, we lost metadata that had to be re-created after the fact. There's no perfect way, and each situation requires a separate analysis.

Mesh Network

The topology of a mesh network is such that every node relays all data for the network and is used when a star topology is too simplistic (see Figure 13.11). Mesh networks are typically wireless and

Figure 13.11	**Mesh topology**

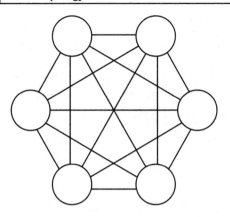

can be deployed in less manicured real-world environments where wireless sensors can fail because of antenna or power issues due to the environment. Mesh networking was developed to operate in these less than optimal conditions where one or more mesh nodes (sensors) can stop operating without impacting the functionality of the network as a whole. This "self-healing" characteristic is also found in IT networks, but a mesh network can communicate without the overhead of a routing table using flooding.

Mesh networking is predominantly used in smart home, smart building, and smart city use cases but is also used in environments where a wired connection is unsafe or impractical, such as inside a pipeline.

The current state of the art in mesh networking is represented by Thread, which employs an open stack utilizing 6LoPAN over 802.15.4 networks. It replaces the antiquated and proprietary ZigBee and Zwave that also run over the 802.15.4 media layer. The other major radio types, cellular, LPWA, Bluetooth, and Wi-Fi, run a star network topology, but efforts are under way to run mesh networks over Bluetooth and Wi-Fi networks.

INFORMATION TECHNOLOGY NETWORK

The IT network is familiar to most people—it's made up of the Internet, the intranet, and all other IT networks (see Figure 13.12). The purpose of the IT network in IoT is to transport data from the OT network to the backhaul link, which transports it to the public and then product cloud. Like OT networks, IT networks can be personal area networks, local area networks, and even wide-area networks. IT network examples include the network connecting the cell tower to fiber infrastructure in smart agriculture and the network connecting the Wi-Fi access point to the metronet for the smart home. It is standardized on IP and is routed, switched, and firewalled using the same network equipment as used in the Internet of People.

Figure 13.12 | **The IT network**

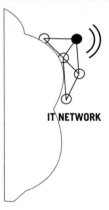

IT NETWORK

FOG LAYER

The fog is the computing, networking, and storage surface that connects the sensor to the uphaul link to the public cloud. Unlike the private and public clouds that reside strictly on IT infrastructure, the fog spans both IT and OT infrastructure (see Figure 13.13).

Figure 13.13	The fog layer

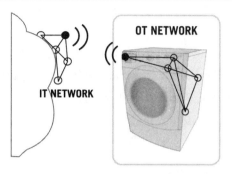

The seam between the two networks is an issue and represents the clash of two worlds: IT and operations. Not only are there technology issues, such as additional attack surfaces threatening security and the extra costs and inefficiencies of protocol conversion gateways; there are human issues. The two different organizations responsible for the fog don't usually have the same business priorities. Whereas IT is constantly changing driven by innovation, operations will resist change, valuing stability and uptime (see Chapter 8 for more details).

Reaching IoT's true potential depends on unifying the fog into one homogeneous network. This means IP must be standardized all the way to the sensor. And just as important, it means that the two teams managing the two networks must be organizationally merged to ensure they are aligned. This is easier when building a greenfield discrete product. Not so much when deploying a brownfield product with an existing infrastructure. It will be this standardization and team consolidation that will overcome this major drag on IoT. Being able to use all the computing resources of the cloud, fog, and embedded and mobile devices allows us to cover all use cases, including those on-prem situations where all computing, networking, and storage must be local.

It should also be noted that mist computing refers to having general computing resources on the embedded systems. Whether the fog rolls over the mist or the mist remains separate is just nomenclature. The network fabric is a distributed computing surface, but the trend is to move the computing as close to the data sources as possible. Among other things, this gives us the option to hoard or not to hoard our data.

To Hoard or Not to Hoard

Within the fog, it takes approximately one-tenth the energy to compute than to communicate—this is important when battery power consumption is an issue. Since only one percent of the data collected is used, it brings into question, how much data should be stored?

This brings us to the topic of data hoarding. Let's say we are collecting data on the friction of the rollers in our home IoT dryer example. We know that as long as the friction is between 0.1 and 0.4 N, the part is operating within specification. The data-hoarding approach is to save all friction data, independent of their value. On the other end of the scale, the data-discarding approach is to perform simple analytics in the fog and only transport and store roller friction data that are greater than 0.4 N or lower than 0.1 N, in other words, the anomalies and the times between anomalies, and discard the rest.

The data-hoarding organization believes that although it is going to be expensive to transport and store all the friction data from all its dryers worldwide, there's gold in dem der hills. In other words, the potential value of the data exhaust is high enough to justify the transport and storage costs and the increased legal risks of keeping it.

Creating new information products is one of the ways to create value with IoT (see Chapter 2 for more details). If you have a plan to sell a subset of the data, then of course you will store it. This conundrum refers more to data you don't have a plan for.

The data-discarding organization has a less romanticized view of data science. It believes data value discovery doesn't happen by accident; it must be planned for from the beginning, and stored data without a plan are just going to collect dust and accrue cost and risk.

There are definite cost savings in being a data discarder, but are they thwarting a future data jackpot? The answer is not Boolean, nor is there a right answer, but in either case, the enterprise needs to have a data strategy for its primary and secondary data.

BACKHAUL

The backhaul connection connects the IT network or fog to the public cloud or Internet.

Connectivity may or may not be included with the product. When connectivity is included, it usually implies cellular, LPWA, or satellite, and a carrier plan must be prenegotiated. This is made more onerous if the product will be sold and used in multiple countries. In those cases, carrier plans must be negotiated individually, country by country, or a backhaul service can be used. Backhaul services do the negotiation for you, consolidating connectivity to one bill and one service-level agreement. These services sometimes include real-time monitoring and billing analytics.

The business situation is significantly less complicated if product connectivity piggybacks atop an existing backhaul connection such as a fixed line connection at the customer's home or workplace via Wi-Fi or wirelessly through the customer's mobile phone via Bluetooth for a wearable product. Less complicated perhaps, but it does have another challenge. The IoT product is now dependent on an infrastructure that's uncontrolled and can be volatile. This may be acceptable for consumer IoT, but it carries a (big) risk for commercial IoT, industrial IoT, and infrastructure IoT.

IOT PRODUCT CLOUD

From the backhaul connection, data travel through the public cloud (the Internet) and are ingested into the private IoT product cloud, which contains the application servers that run the non-resident application and databases (see Figure 13.14). There are IoT clouds, and there are IT clouds. Most readers are familiar with IT clouds.

The cloud-as-a-service business model has transformed IT, with most enterprises today having a public cloud component of their IT strategy. Like the IT cloud, the IoT cloud is used for computation, communication, and storage, greatly increasing the functionality and performance of the IoT product. While similar in nature, the IoT cloud differs in two important regards: tech and business.

Figure 13.14 | **The IoT product cloud**

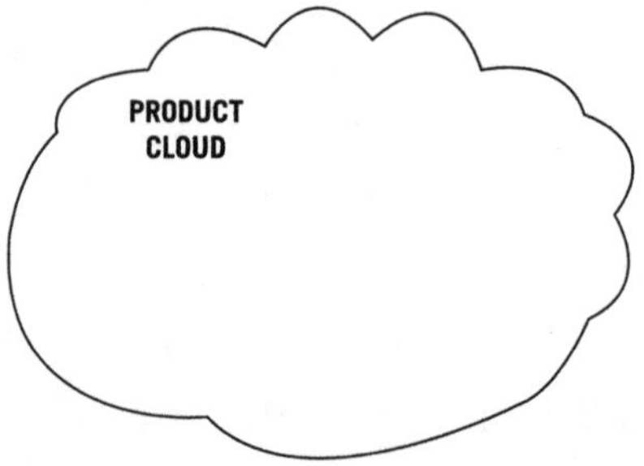

PRODUCT
CLOUD

The IoT cloud differs in that it must support the application protocols and analytics packages most popularly used by IoT products. Like the IT cloud, it should also interface with the most popular PLM, CRM, and ERP business systems. The IoT cloud must also interface with your company's development tools of choice for building cybermodels and applications, as well as interface with the APIs of the data services you may need such as weather, mapping, pricing, etc.

Besides being compatible with the technical components of an IoT product, its business model must be compatible with the velocity, variety, and volume of data found in IoT. Data from sensors and external services in IoT differ from what are typically found in IT. In general, there are more connections sending smaller amounts of data in more formats. If the IoT cloud business model charges by number of connections, as is the case for cellular human plans, the costs will be too high.

IOT PLATFORM

I always recommend to my clients to buy or lease an IoT platform (see Figure 13.15). This goes back to core competencies and intellectual property. IoT platforms are the plumbing of IoT—middleware software packaging some or all of the IoT cloud, a development environment, IT network software, and sometimes OT network software and even small agent hardware, all wrapped within a security framework. The purpose of the IoT platform is to transport sensor and external system data to the application where they can be acted upon and analyzed to create value. Unless a core competency of your company is or must be networking, then it doesn't make sense to create your own unique intellectual property here.

Figure 13.15	The IoT platform

Types

There are hundreds of commercial IoT platforms available, generally classified into one of three types: application enablement platforms (AEPs), provisioning platforms, and connectivity platforms. AEPs provide a more holistic and encompassing environment to develop an IoT product. These platforms are used in consumer, commercial, industrial, and infrastructure IoT. Provisioning platforms are used to bring online and manage communication radios—generally cellular but also LPWA and satellite. Their history is in M2M and telematics, but their reach is expanding. Connectivity platforms generally connect a product on an OT network to a cloud and that cloud to a mobile device. Connectivity to the OT network is accomplished through a software agent that runs on existing popular embedded systems or on the platform's own embedded hardware. Consumer and commercial IoT use these platforms to connect a product to a mobile device, which by itself does not create enough value, at least from my perspective.

Specialty

Beyond type, the next way to narrow your IoT platform choices is by industry specialty. Over time, common platform functionality will become commoditized, leaving industry specificity as a differentiator. Oil and gas platforms will differ from smart agriculture platforms, which will differ from logistics platforms. They will differ not by how the plumbing is made—that will be the commoditized part—but by how the analytics and development environments are tailored to specific industry needs, and possibly OT network integration, but that's rare. Over time, every industry vertical will consolidate into one to three platforms. These may be mostly customized versions of fewer common platforms, but that's still a lot of platforms.

Architecture

Platform architecture is yet another way to narrow your choices. Roughly mapping onto application protocols, there is a spectrum of choices based on the degree of responsiveness needed. Message-based architectures are generally not as responsive as client-server–based architectures but can be less complicated to manage and maintain. So the question becomes, how "real-time" does your product need to be? All things being equal, platforms based on a messaging application protocol such as MQTT will not be as responsive as those based on a client-server protocol such as DDS.

Commercial Versus Open Source

A final way to differentiate IoT platforms is open source versus commercial. At this time, open-source IoT platforms are not as functionally rich nor are they as robust, especially at scale, as their commercial counterparts. This I believe will change, and with this change will be a movement to open-source platforms. When buying into a commercial platform, your product's existence depends on it. If the controlling entity has a change in strategy or goes out of business, that's a problem, a problem that makes open-source software more attractive. I certainly would not wait for open source, but there are precautions you can take while working with a commercial platform vendor.

Ensure you have an escrow provision in your contract for the source code and keys. Although not perfect, this will help in the unfortunate event that you find yourself with unsupported or, worse, bricked middleware. But realistically speaking, if that doomed day were to come, taking on the responsibility of maintaining this significant piece of code is generally an issue. Better is to design a technical exit from the start. Avoid hard-coding any extensions and stick to known protocols. Modularize your software architecture so that all the intellectual property important to your organization, such as everything related to the app, model, and analytics, is isolated by its own API in a way that can be plugged into any platform. Like security, designing modularity into the architecture up front is infinitely easier than having to face this dreaded issue after the fact. This is a general best practice.

Recommendations

All enterprises should use an IoT platform, no matter what industry they are in, what their product does, and what stage of development they are in. The business model of leasing an IoT platform scales with usage based on the number of calls made, the number of bits moved, the number of bits stored, etc. During the early stages of development, platforms provide a rich set of low-cost tools to get to a proof of concept or prototype. Costs increase only as customers use your product, increasing your revenue. This is a small price to pay when considering how difficult and expensive it would be to build and scale this plumbing internally. But remember to have an exit strategy.

Platforms today are used to build single IoT products and IoT product lines, but the end goal is for platforms to support product lines from multiple organizations in support of building ecosystems (see Chapter 7 for more details).

• • •

Now that we have the plumbing under control, we next look at external systems that will feed data in and out of these pipes.

EXTERNAL SYSTEMS INCLUDING OTHER IOT PRODUCTS

Interfacing with external systems is what mainly differentiates the IoT product from the connected product and smart product. The IoT product interfaces with the Internet in the same way web software and mobile apps do today (see Figure 14.1). This makes available massive functionality for relatively low effort, and in the process, it completely changes what a physical product can do.

When I started my career as a programmer, I had to develop almost everything from the ground up. With the exception of using graphics hardware libraries, everything was written from scratch. While good from a flexibility and learning perspective, it was slow. Gratifying but slow. Today's Internet programmers can more easily stand on the shoulders of their predecessors, accessing the numerous libraries of prewritten functionality with relatively simple APIs. A lot of what you need today is either already out there or can be quickly put together from existing parts. This explains why sophisticated mobile apps and websites can be developed so quickly. IoT products can enjoy all the same benefits.

All incremental value of an IoT product comes from transforming its data into useful information. When most people think

Figure 14.1	External systems as part of the IoT product

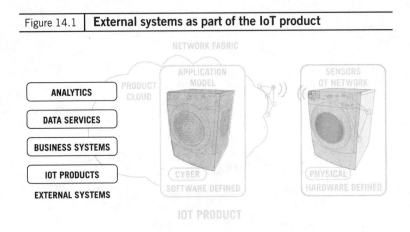

of IoT data, they think of sensors, but it's much more than that. External systems provide external sources of data in addition to the data that come in from internal sensors (see Figure 14.2). These data can be raw or may be preprocessed into information. External systems come in four main categories:

- Analytics

- Data services

- Business systems

- Other IoT products

Analytics is different and very important. As such, it is extensively covered in the next chapter. Before we dive into analytics, let's focus on the other three external systems.

DATA SERVICES

Data microservices are abundant on the Internet. For a reasonable fee, or sometimes for free, your software can tap into data on

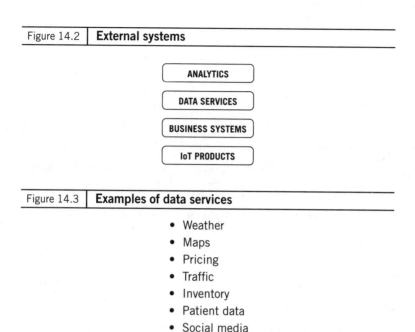

Figure 14.2 | **External systems**

ANALYTICS

DATA SERVICES

BUSINESS SYSTEMS

IoT PRODUCTS

Figure 14.3 | **Examples of data services**

- Weather
- Maps
- Pricing
- Traffic
- Inventory
- Patient data
- Social media
- Commodity data

everything from weather to maps to stock prices (see Figure 14.3). If data are the new oil, data services are the new oil rigs on the Internet horizon.

These data are valuable. Consider IBM's purchase of the Weather Company for a reported $3.3 billion. IBM is a tech bellwether, always a step ahead of the computing industry, as demonstrated by its transformation from hardware provider to software developer to services consultancy and now to data vendor. Data are becoming increasingly valuable, as demonstrated by IBM's acquisitions and its companywide focus on Watson.

BUSINESS SYSTEMS

As business processes change, so too will how we update and access our business systems. IoT can directly interface with the enterprise's business systems. This is not only to pull out useful data on a customer's business but to populate these systems with product, customer, and business data ingested by the IoT product.

All enterprises can use this data gathered to improve operations. The data could be for sales (via CRM) to quantify and target their customer's needs, from suppliers (via SCM) to anticipate manufacturing needs, about internal resources (via ERP) to optimize maintenance spending and resource allocation, or for product management (via PLM) to capture insights on how customers want to use their products today and in the future.

Each business system is accessed through its API. The API is used either to put data (and information) generated by your IoT product into your business or to get data to be used by your product to improve innovation, operational efficiency, asset utilization, and invention.

OTHER IOT PRODUCTS

As we have discussed, an IoT product is an intraconnected system of systems. But when value really starts bending the curve is when IoT products are connected to other IoT products, using each other as sources of data. The IoT Tech Continuum, as discussed in Chapter 5, will be one of the two main trends (the other being the IoT Business Model Continuum) enabling ecosystems, outcomes, and ultimately the Outcome Economy by connecting more and more products to each other.

An IoT product as an external data system is extremely powerful. This IoT product can be from the same product line or from a different company's product line that shares a common IoT platform. The ability to orchestrate disparate products to provide customer outcomes will broaden the definition of how products work and how they work together. But most importantly it increases value.

As Metcalfe's law applies to the value of a network, so too does it apply to the value of a network of products, which increases exponentially when connected (see Chapter 7 for a derivation). With IoT products you should think beyond the individual product and consider how multiple products can work together. Because they can. Because they can and because this increases value, if you are not going to connect them, your competitors will.

• • •

Using analytics on the big data generated by IoT is a game changer and along with the model and application of the software-defined product, creates all the value in the Internet of Things. The next chapter dives into this supremely important tech.

IOT ANALYTICS
AND BIG DATA

Big data sets are commonplace in IoT, where the normalizing dimension is time. Big data, small data—no matter what the size, analyzing data is core to the Internet of Things. In all forms of analytics there are two main components: the data and the model. Data come from sensors, generally in time series form, and from external systems in unstructured form. Data define and improve the model and are compared with the model in different ways to provide insights. Depending on the task at hand, analytics can live anywhere on the compute surface: the public cloud, the private cloud, and the fog, and the analytics can even live in the mist (the embedded system).

THE DIFFERENT TYPES OF ANALYTICS

Given the nature of IoT data, I like to categorize the analytics based on the dimension of time, answering these three questions (see Figure 15.1):

Figure 15.1	Categorizing analytics by time

Past	Present	Future
Descriptive	Rules Engine	Predictive
Diagnostic	RT Analysis	Prescriptive

→

Time

What happened?	What is happening?	What could happen?
Why did it happen?		What should happen?

1. What happened in the past?

2. What's happening in the present?

3. What's going to happen in the future?

What Happened?

Descriptive analytics and diagnostic analytics are used to answer the questions, what happened and why did it happen? Both forms of data mining wade through the data to understand what happened in the past, but they do so in different ways.

Descriptive analytics uses visualization to display the data in ways that help human brains pick out the subtleties difficult to identify and convey through mathematics alone. The concept is not new. My first company, Wavefront, sold a product called the Data Visualizer to scientists and engineers. More recently we've seen this kind of functionality with business intelligence (BI) software, generally used in business. Descriptive analytics is a continuation of this class of software, dedicated to visualizing data captured, in this case by the IoT product.

Seeing things visually is often easier to comprehend than viewing a bunch of 2D graphs, or worse, a bunch of matrices. For example, coloring the 3D model of a bucket wheel excavator with stress and strain information gathered by its sensors and animated over time is an efficient way to convey hot spots and areas to study after a structure or joint failed. This technique works well when dealing with five or fewer dimensions; however, when the analysis is of higher order, it is difficult and time consuming to prep and then display the data in a way that is comprehensible. Augmented reality and virtual reality are natural display techniques for descriptive analytics that can likely increase the dimensionality of visualization beyond five.

Diagnostic analytics is used in multidimensional situations and in more general situations when you're diagnosing a problem by solving or optimizing the model in the context of the data at hand. Following on the excavator example, diagnostic analytics would be well used to compare the simulated data used in CAD with the real data collected using the Internet of Things. What would be mindboggling using descriptive analytics can be routinely handled in multidimensions by diagnostic analytics.

Diagnostic analytics uses the various fields of data mining to discover important facts, trends, patterns, and abnormalities that may have gone unrecognized by simply looking at numbers, graphs, or visualizations.

What's Happening?

While analytics that focuses on the past or future considers data at rest, working in the present means that the data being analyzed are in motion. This constrains where the analysis can be performed and the type of analysis that can be performed. Although data analysis in the present isn't necessarily real time, the latency involved in data traveling to the public cloud and back generally excludes that cloud as a compute surface. Rules engines and stream processing are performed closer to the data source and answer the question, what's happening?

Rules engines can be stand-alone but are typically found within competitive AEP IoT platforms. Stream processing can be part of the application or executed by an external system interfaced with the application. In either case, computing is performed by a server on prem; by a router, switch, or gateway in the fog; or by an embedded system at the edge.

"Real-time" analytics, or better classified as run-time analytics, computes logical or functional relationships between incoming data and a model or variables of a model. This is powered by simple pattern recognition and pattern matching and can be used for filtering and windowing—comparing if numbers or functions are between other numbers or functions. An example is checking to see if the heating element in the IoT dryer is too hot—capturing "abnormal" data to send to the cloud for data mining versus discarding data after they're considered "normal."

What's Going to Happen?

The heavyweights of analytics can predict the future. Predictive analytics answers the question, what can happen?, and prescriptive analytics answers the question, what should happen? The difference between the two is that prescriptive analytics goes one step further. After deciding what is going to happen, prescriptive analytics compares its prediction with the desired outcome and then works backward to understand what changes need to be made to course-correct the product to the desired result. These changes require closing the loop, that is, being able to make updates to the software and modifying the physical product through actuation.

My dryer is old, at least 10 years old, maybe older, but it works just fine. That wasn't always the case. About two years ago it started letting out a little squeak now and then. Not so bad, easy enough to ignore, so that's what we did; we attributed the squeaking to our dryer's quirky personality and ignored it. But overnight it went from a cute squeak every now and then to a full-time shrilling scream whenever the dryer was on. It was so bad that we resigned ourselves to having to buy a replacement. Something that loud and horrible sounding, combined with the dryer's age, had to be fatal. While looking online for a new replacement, I thought I'd do a cryptic search: "Maytag dryer loud squeak," and sure enough, it was a common problem. And after further investigation I found the trouble, which was curable by replacing the simple set of $10 rollers the drum rests on. All I had to do was pull the dryer out from its tight quarters, disassemble it, and replace the worn-out parts. After a few tries, closely following a couple of YouTube videos, I had it back together. To this day there's a satisfying purr whenever our dryer is on.

Had my dryer been an IoT dryer, predictive analytics could have identified the change in the rolling friction of my rollers to alert me, based on cumulative past events, that my rollers were going to start squeaking. If I had had a predictive maintenance service, it would have given me the chance to call my repairperson or buy the $10 parts online before the annoyance began. And if my IoT dryer had prescriptive analytics, it could not only recognize the impending squeaking problem but try to prevent it from happening. In this fictitious example it would actuate the dryer's roller lubricators to reduce the friction, thereby averting the loud noise or at least postponing it to some time in the future.

It's one thing that predictive and prescriptive maintenance is possible, but it's quite another thing for the manufacturer to develop and offer it. It depends on how it's going to be monetized. Referring back to Chapter 3, if the product business model is used, this type of service will not be made available to me since the manufacturer's business is to sell $1,000 products, not $10 parts. If I purchased this as an add-on service, sold as part of the product-service business model, the service would notify me of the problem (as in the above example). If the IoT dryer is sold using the service business model, the manufacturer would be notified of the impending problem and come to my home to service it.

Which Type of Analytics Package Do You Choose?

The selection of an analytics package comes down to whether you are looking into the past, present, or future, which we covered earlier. Then you must consider the characteristics of the data you're processing; these are the so-called volume, velocity, and variety of the data, where volume dictates parallel or nonparallel processing, velocity dictates in-memory (RAM) or not in-memory processing, and variety dictates the need to work with a structured or nonstructured database. The last decision to make when selecting your analytics is whether to choose an open-source or commercial (closed-source) package. Commercial products change over time, and so I do not list their names in this book; but to get an updated list, search for the *Iot-Inc Buyer's Guide*, or go to http://www.iot-inc .com/buyers-guide to find the latest commercial analytics products.

HOW ANALYTICS IS DONE

So how is analytics performed? How do you do it? It's a three-step process: getting things ready, crunching numbers, and then reporting the results (see Figure 15.2).

Figure 15.2	**Analytics steps**

1. Extract, transform, load (ETL)—data preparation in database
2. Processing (analysis)
3. Report, visualization, action

Step 1: Getting Things Ready

If there is a sexy part of data science, step 1 isn't it. Prepping the data, what is called ETL—extract, transform, and load— usually takes at least 75 percent of the data scientist's time. This entails:

- Identifying and then pulling out data, in their native format, from a data lake and transferring the data into logically separate and hierarchical data pools

- Normalizing the data's different parts to match structure and time and then massaging the data into a form that is compatible with the analytics package

- Loading (or pointing to) the data for the database to start the analysis

Maybe you have done this with Excel; you know, getting data into a form that can be graphed for a report you worked on: deleting columns, changing certain cells from text into real numbers, adding rows of data from other files, eliminating duplicates . . . you get the picture. Data wrangling isn't sexy, but it's where data scientists or their helpers spend a majority of their time.

Step 2: Number Crunching

The first step in crunching numbers is selecting the right equations, or more accurately, classes of equations, to apply to your data: equations that incorporate the variables of your model and provide a good fit for the data extracted. Choosing the best class of equations can be as much an art as a science. And increasingly the science being used to help data scientists make the selection of the best equation class is machine learning. After defining the data set and setting up its parameters, the data analysts define the analytics they want to perform and hit "go." Maybe the analysts are using a graphic interface, or maybe it's a command line interface, but in either case, this starts the process of number crunching, so to speak, in order to answer what happened or what's going to happen. In the "How It Works" section below, we discuss the number crunching in more detail.

Step 3: Communicating the Results

After the analysis is complete, some mechanism is used to communicate the results. This can be with descriptive analytics to produce a visualization, with BI to produce more recognizable graphs, or with an analytical report.

DATABASES AND DIFFERENT TYPES OF DATA

Databases hold the data gathered from the sensors and external systems in a contextual way. The entire set of raw data, stored in their original format and in a flat hierarchy, is referred to as a data lake. Data pools, as referred to in the previous section, are portions of the lake that have been logically separated and transformed to be acted upon by an analytics event.

Data can be nicely structured in rows and columns or unstructured, consisting of different types of data that may have parts missing (sparse). IoT sensor data are generally correlated by time, which is why IoT data are often referred to as time series data. It is the dimension of time that brings together the cyberworld with the physical world.

Databases are chosen to match the analytics package, or they're included with the package. In either case the databases will match the volume, velocity, and variety of the data. For projects with static outputs, that is, for analytics looking into the past or future, database structures are almost as nice and clean as described here. However, for analytics with dynamic outputs such as for real-time optimizations or any streaming process that needs to update models, database structures are messier and require customization to solve specific problems.

HOW ANALYTICS WORKS

This section describes how analytics works. Not the mathematics involved, but the concepts at hand. As you will see, how analytics works is pretty simple. However, the mathematics behind the concepts, which you won't see, are anything but simple. Complexity arises due to the number of variables involved— the so-called curse of dimensionality. If there are 100 sensors involved, then we could be dealing with equations with up to 100 degrees of freedom. While the equations are computationally easy to solve, issues arise because the interactions among subsystems grow exponentially.

If that sounds like a complex model, it's because it is; but now consider that we may have hundreds if not thousands of models associated at the part, product, or system level and consider that each model may have more than 100 variables or orders of magnitude more. This is the definition of big data.

At a high level, there aren't that many types of fundamental analytics operations. You are either building or updating the model, comparing the model, or solving the model in some way by isolating variables, by optimizing, or by finding trends. Let's take a look inside.

Build and Update

All analytics starts with a model. The model is first built and then iterated upon to improve it over time (see Figure 15.3). The focus of the model can be at any level: at the part, product, product line, or ecosystem level. The class of model depends on the type of analytics it's for: descriptive, diagnostic, rules engine, stream processing, predictive, or prescriptive. And all models encompass variables like the ones we identified in our example models, to be compared, matched, or optimized or solved for.

The data scientists, increasingly with machine learning, choose the stochastic model class (type of equation) to be used to represent the product's data in a higher-level form. Think of this as the skeletal frame of the model. To increase the accuracy of the model, data are needed. Lots of data. Each data stream is associated with a variable. And each data stream can come from the sensors of the hardware-defined product or from external systems such as data services, business systems, and other IoT products. Since it is an iterative process, the quality of the model improves with time.

In our IoT dryer example, the focus of the model is at the product level. In this case we have two families of models. The first will be to define drying time, and the second will be to describe the cost savings. The streams that provide the data to improve model

---

| Figure 15.3 | **Build and update model** |

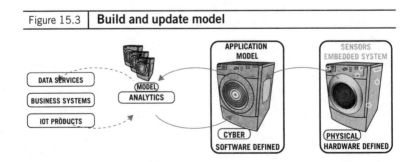

quality come from sensing fan speed, angular velocity, heater temperature, drum temperature, and load weight. Energy pricing will come from a data service hosted by the local utility. And remember, these six data streams will include metadata to contextualize the payload. This can include the units of measure, the machine, the state of the machine, and possibly the state of the environment it's in. It should also include data on the software and hardware capturing the data, to be used as "bread crumbs" in the event that we need to identify "dirty data" or any other "ghost in the machine."

Compare or Match

Anomaly detection, a subset of pattern recognition, which is a subset of machine learning, is employed in IoT in all classes of analytics but in different ways. In general, model variables or equations of model variables are mathematically compared for equivalency or ranges of equivalency (see Figure 15.4).

In the example of the clothes dryer, we can apply anomaly detection to the friction coefficient measured in the roller bearing. In this one-dimensional case, the anomaly is detected by stream analysis if the coefficient is higher than a predefined threshold. Since it is abnormal for the friction coefficient to be higher than, say, 0.35, when 0.36 is detected, it triggers an action such as sending a message or lubricating the bearings. This can also be used to drive descriptive analytics to graphically display any model variable that is out of the norm. This example is one-dimensional (1D), so it only gets more mathematically intense from here.

In Figure 15.4, we are comparing two 2D curves with each other. In predictive analytics and prescriptive analytics, this comparison is the key function. Let's say we want to predict if a dryer roller needs to be replaced because of squeaking. The first step is to associate the two variables of friction (cause) and time to the out-

Figure 15.4 | Compare model

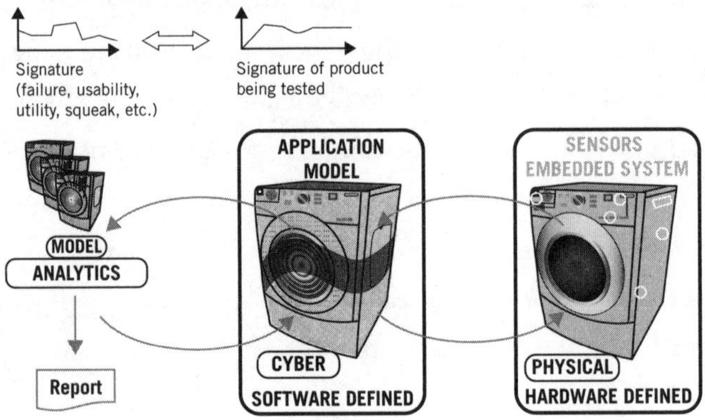

come of squeaking (effect). Over time and over many IoT dryers, we capture these two variables for all dryers and examine the data sets of dryers that had rollers that started squeaking.

By sampling more and more dryers that squeak, we build up a progressively more accurate 2D squeak signature. To determine if a given dryer is going to squeak, we compare its "squeak signature" with the master squeak model's "squeak signature." If the two signatures are close, we can predict that the machine will start squeaking with a level of confidence based on how close the signatures are.

The reason analytics is so computationally intensive is because we don't limit ourselves to comparing patterns in one or two dimensions. These models can have hundreds or even thousands of dimensions (variables) and could look across hundreds or even thousands of machines. Computing with these multidimensional models is where the heavy lifting and heavy mathematics come in. Helping things along is data scientist intelligence plus artificial intelligence to determine the definition of a match.

Let's look at an example of how pattern recognition can be used in our clothes dryer in usability and utility modeling. Usability has been done for ages with websites. An interface is designed based on how the designer expects the website to be used. To analyze the difference between how the website was designed to be used versus how it is actually used, a model with variables such as a task time, button clicks, etc., is set up with analytics. The difference between the expectation and reality models can be quantified to help improve the product's usability.

The same concept applies to the clothes dryer. The usability model, being refined by thousands of product owners, can inform the IoT dryer manufacturer on how to make its product more usable. The same can be done for utility—comparing what you expect the product will be used for with what it's actually used for, e.g., expected load size.

Solve, Optimize, Find Trends

This is a postprocess that does not require new data, only the model (see Figure 15.5). Since models are mathematical equations, we can solve them in different ways. We could isolate one or more variables and solve for them based on the other variables. For example, how much electricity does it take to dry a particular load? Or we could optimize (minimize or maximize) an equation. For example, given this load of laundry, what's the shortest amount of time to dry it, and what are the variable values used (e.g., drum

| Figure 15.5 | Solve, optimize, trend model |

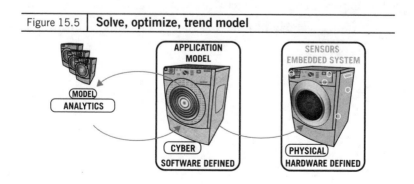

speed, fan speed, and heater temperature) to actuate in the physical IoT dryer to make this happen?

Trending insights could come from many similar products; for example, the most popular time to dry clothes could be calculated mathematically with regression analysis.

Another mathematical technique is to reverse engineer a desired result. Let me explain. If after a certain amount of data collection, say we discover the perfect configuration of the IoT dryer to minimize drying time while maintaining the integrity of the clothes (not shrinking, stretching, or wrinkling); in other words, we identify the perfect coefficients of the model's variables to minimize drying time for different loads. Then we can work backward, and for any given load, we can calculate the variables to get this same result; i.e., for any given load we can calculate how to set the dryer's drum speed, fan speed, and heater temperature.

Of course, optimization is not static as presented here. In the future, and in some cases already today, we can close the loop with the model to keep optimizing it through our application each time we do a load.

• • •

Analytics is key to value creation—one of the trio of value, along with the model and application. However, we will not get a chance to create value unless our IoT products are safe and secure. The next chapter covers cybersecurity (technology) in the context of risk (business), which must be considered from the start of any IoT product's design.

CHAPTER 16

IOT CYBERSECURITY AND RISK MANAGEMENT

The lack of security is said to be one of the biggest friction points holding back the adoption of the Internet of Things, and I can understand that. Fear sells, and for the press it's easier to attract a link click when talking about all the things that can go wrong in IoT. When products or systems or environments go haywire, people and assets can get hurt and damaged, but I don't subscribe to this fearmongering. We've been doing cybersecurity for over five decades. Have things gone wrong? Sure, but we have adapted. While we will never be fully cybersecure in IoT, we have already adapted to this reality. Something bad happens, and then we figure out how to stop it from happening again. Have there been some big, costly, and embarrassing hacks to our IT infrastructure? Sure, and we have adapted. But are banks, the richest of targets, being emptied of their money on a daily basis? No, because over time we figure it out.

History will repeat itself with IoT. Will there be as many high-profile hacks to the physical world? Sure, probably worse, but we'll adapt to the new normal, and we'll figure it out one step at a time. The IoT industry is still small, and despite the hype, it's growing slowly and methodologically. We'll hit roadblocks, but the whole time we will be learning along the way, progressively releasing safer and safer IoT products.

In this book I mostly take a business approach to IoT and IoT security; after all, that's the point of the book. But in those areas where capitalism may weigh profit above human safety or national security, we must recognize that government too has a role to play. Legislation and regulation will and should be applied commensurate with the risk to safety and security in consumer, commercial, and industrial IoT, but especially in infrastructure IoT, as it pertains to critical communication, transportation (rail, air, road), and power (production and distribution). Successful attacks in these areas can have worse ramifications than our largest industrial accidents and natural disasters. But these stem from malicious human intent, intent that we are battling.

The above caveat and my own fearmongering notwithstanding, to effectively fight cybercrime, we must recognize from the start that this is not a technical problem but a business one. Technical cybersecurity will only be effective if directed and funded by the business and the discipline of risk management.

HOW MUCH IS SECURITY WORTH TO YOU?

Being an information technology, IoT is vulnerable to the same cyber threats as IT: threats to the confidentiality of its data, threats to the integrity of its data, and threats to the accessibility of its data. Threats to IoT's data at rest are for the most part no different from those faced in IT. However, as a data-collecting machine, IoT faces unique threats to its data in motion. Cybersecurity is never finished, never working perfectly, and always having to be improved. Cybersecurity is a problem of budget. For every threat, there is a risk, and every risk has a price tag to mitigate it.

Pushing back on the need for better cybersecurity is a real lack of demand. Unfortunately, consumers and therefore product managers prioritize security low on their wish list. When the choice is between security and convenience, convenience always wins. When the choice is between security and the metaphorical bells and whistles, the bells and whistles win every time. The demand today for IoT security is lower than that for IT security even though the ramifications of a security breach could be higher. This is probably due to the relative immaturity of the industry as compared with IT and the relative immaturity of IoT-related attacks.

If it's not consumer and business demand, what's going to drive better security? A catastrophic event? Government intervention? Standardization or better training? No one knows for sure what will cause the change, but I think it will be time. Eventually the level of security and tolerable risk will equalize.

THREATS AND SOURCES OF LIABILITY

All incremental value of an IoT product comes from transforming its data into useful information. Therefore, a company's IoT assets are its data and information (abbreviated to data for the rest of this chapter). These assets must be protected because of their value and the potential liability they represent. Let's start by looking at the threats and liabilities, then in the second half of this chapter we'll look at how to balance these threats and liabilities with risk management.

Data Confidentiality

Threats to the confidentiality of IoT data are similar to those in IT with the exception of the new threat vector pointing at data in motion within the OT network. Defensive cybersecurity ensures that the data get to the right place and do not fall into the wrong hands. Traditional IT security methods, such as encryption, perimeter control, and social engineering education, protect against such threats.

Liability here is associated with user privacy, loss of company intellectual property, and the public tarnishing of the company's brand. The access to customer personally identifiable information is a source of legal liability, especially in B2C IoT. In B2B IoT, PII is less of an issue than the competitive liability or the legal liability associated with the loss of customer business operations data.

Data Integrity

Integrity refers to the trustworthiness and accuracy of the data. Data must not be corrupted or changed, so security for access control and data inspection is employed to ensure the validity of the information and the information source. Another, more recent tool to safeguard OT networks uses analytics to examine network traffic to compare it with "normal" network traffic. Given that the nodes in the OT network are things rather than people, the traffic patterns are more limited and predictable and therefore easier to establish and recognize than in the IT network.

Liability here is mostly associated with data in motion in the OT network. If a bad actor modifies existing data or injects new data, he or she can crash the IoT product, make it inoperable, or make it act erratically. Bad actors can instruct the product to carry out the wrong action, or even more worrisome, they can take control of the system. In the virtual IT world, this has financial ramifications, but in the physical IoT world, this can put human lives at risk. The loss of data integrity puts the company in danger of potentially existential liability.

Data Availability

Availability refers to the reliability of access to the data and product by authorized users. As on the web, a denial of service or distributed denial of service (DDoS) attack can overwhelm the IoT product, causing it to cease operating. Unfortunately, the same accessible and affordable tools used to bring down a website can be used to bring down any external web interface in IoT, especially problematic when on the critical path of operating an IoT product. While websites can employ "heavy iron" DDoS intercept security solutions on their front end, this is typically not a practical option for IoT.

Making an IoT product unavailable can bring with it direct liabilities such as breach of contract or indirect liabilities, both of which can result in having to defend against legal action. Consider the fallout of a DDoS attack on a web authentication service if that were the only way for the crew members of the $100 million Bagger 293 to log in to start their shift and operate the machine.

THE SIX ATTACK VECTORS OF IOT SECURITY

As we know, an IoT product is not a discrete entity but a system of systems. Attack vectors usually target the interfaces between systems. While software provides the IoT product all its advantages, it's also responsible for the security disadvantages, found at the programming interfaces between systems. The implication is

Figure 16.1 | **Attack vectors in IoT**

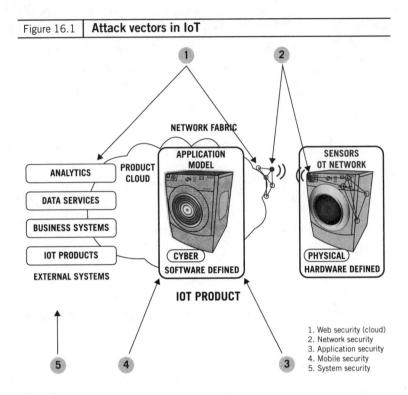

1. Web security (cloud)
2. Network security
3. Application security
4. Mobile security
5. System security

that there are multiple disciplines of cybersecurity involved. Let's discuss them in the order of the data flow from the sensor (see Figure 16.1).

Physical Security

The embedded system's SWaP (size, weight, and power) constraints makes securing the end nodes challenging. Debug interfaces, such as JTAG, are perfect ingress points, as are bootloaders. If the attacker gets access to the firmware, the attacker owns the device.

Sensors, actuators, and gateways are also physically exposed to the world. As such, physical tampering can possibly extract data, inject data, or stop data from flowing, forcing vendors to make their physical enclosures strong and sound.

Network Security

OT and IT networks are vulnerable to the same networking attacks we protect against in the Internet of People. Uniquely vulnerable in IoT, however, is the IT-OT seam that separates the two networks. This physically manifests itself as a gateway that translates proprietary OT protocols into the Internet protocol—and in the process provides a convenient attack location. Also the OT network is more likely to be physically exposed than its IT counterpart.

Cloud and Web Security

Any connection with the public cloud or with web services introduces vulnerabilities originating from third-party APIs and their authentication method. For an IoT product this is found at the uplink to the public cloud and between the product and any external service or database.

Application Security

Your application code is secured by the physical, network, and cloud and web security just mentioned, but the application server is also a target. Access to the application is through its API. External third-party apps are protected by security frameworks that are mostly out of your control, but your application is a different story. Pay extra attention to secure your custom API, especially problematic if executed on premise.

Mobile Security

In addition to living on the embedded system, network nodes, cloud, and application server, an app also often lives on the mobile device, exposing yet another attack surface. While there are several on-device security issues to be concerned about, most mobile security concerns are limited to the RESTful API end point used for authentication, authorization, etc.

System Security

So far we've considered five classes of attack surfaces. That's a lot. And while it's tough enough to look at each surface in isolation, when brought together in IoT, there is a new class of vulnerability introduced related to the system security. System security is needed to ensure one system doesn't inadvertently introduce a vulnerability into another. Consider system A and system B, which can be almost any combination of physical, network, cloud, application, and mobile. A common vulnerability arises when access to system B through system A is open because system B does not enforce its own authentication since it incorrectly assumes that system A already authenticated the user. Security interdependencies must be examined.

SECURITY BEST PRACTICES

The first IoT security best practice is to utilize the software development life cycle (SDLC) approach to security within your organization. The SDLC approach incorporates security into the ideation, design, development, testing, and release phases of the software development life cycle. I will briefly discuss these phases here, highlighting relevant security best practices along the way.

Ideation

Define security features and security requirements for your model, application, and analytics while defining your product's other requirements during the concept and ideation phase. This was discussed in Chapter 9, "Defining Your IoT Product's Requirements."

Design

"Security by design" refers to designing in security from the ground up so that important functionality does not have to be "bolted on" later, as retrofitting security is a recipe for disaster. It's telling that the first thing external security experts request, after being brought in due to a breach, is to see the security design architecture. Without an explicit architecture, there is no plan. Without a plan, there is no effective security.

Security by design is performed during the risk management process, which comprises the second half of this chapter.

Development

During development, best practices include using security frameworks as intended, using network segmentation, implementing OTA update delivery, encrypting (almost) everything, and taking an honest internal skill inventory, each of which we will review below.

Use Security Frameworks as Intended

Security frameworks of one form or another are publicly available for network security, web security, mobile security, cryptography, etc. First off, use them. There's no reason, for example, to develop your own authentication code when there are so many battle-tested (and open) authentication frameworks out there. Second, when you do use them, use them as they're configured to be used. Many a postbreach autopsy has discovered that security personnel had modified a framework. Through ignorance or with the best of intentions, not using security frameworks as intended could have the dire unintended consequence of opening systems up to unknown vulnerabilities.

Use Network Segmentation

An air gap is the strongest form of protection. For example, keeping your IoT automobile's entertainment network separate from its navigation network just makes common sense. Or does it? In this case yes, but a lot of IoT's value is about interconnectivity and intraconnectivity, so a balance with network segmentation must be made. Double sensing can be used to get the value of merging networks with the security of an air gap. Double sensing is having identical sensors on separate air-gapped networks. It's redundant and costs more, but the value can be high.

Implement an OTA Update Delivery System

Cybersecurity is an ongoing cat-and-mouse game with the bad actors always one step ahead. Vulnerabilities are exploited, then discovered, and then patched. It's a continuous cycle you must tap into by subscribing to these security patches. What's astounding is, for 99.9 percent of exploited vulnerabilities resulting in successful attacks, not only was the type of attack known, but a patch had been available to prevent it for at least a year. According to the FTC, 999 attack types of 1,000 can be thwarted by keeping your security code up-to-date. Incorporating these patches is the hard part. What's required is an over-the-air patch update system. But implementing it in a way that does not impede the practical use of your product is challenging. And consider too that an OTA system is also an attack surface in itself.

Encrypt (Almost) Everything

In theory, if you use end-to-end encryption, you maintain the confidentiality of your data, even if your system is breached. But like everything else in security, the devil is in the details, or maybe better put, the devil is in the humans that implement the encryption. Mistakes are made. For example, if you don't secure and manage the encryption keys properly, the lock can be opened. For an added price, current embedded systems can be equipped with the computational power needed to encrypt, but is it needed? If the liability is low, then it may not be necessary to encrypt all data. This can only be answered by doing a risk assessment, which will be discussed later in the chapter.

Take an Honest Internal Skill Inventory

Let's be real here; with the far-reaching needs of IoT security, it's difficult, if not impossible, to have people knowledgeable enough about network, web, application, mobile, and system security to keep your product safe. The thing about developers (I know, because I was one) is that they often overestimate their strengths and underestimate the energy required to complete a programming project, especially a project they are less familiar with. Security is no different. Security gaps will be present, and don't assume security skills are transferable. Identify the gaps and fill them with specialized resources. Take an honest inventory of your internal capabilities. If help can't be found internally or recruited in a timely manner, it can be found in external security firms.

Testing

Testing includes both vulnerability scanning using equipment and penetration testing using an internal or external team.

Pen Testing

One of the most effective testing techniques is called pen testing, or penetration testing. Pen testing is a set of ethical hacking techniques designed to expose vulnerabilities in the data network. If you attempt to hack into the IoT system without any more information than the typical bad actor has, you are acting like you're wearing a black hat and are working on a black box. If you are given the backstory and all the resources of an internal team, then you are wearing a white hat and working on a white box. A gray hat means you do a little of both, starting with a black hat and then switching it off for a white one. This third approach is often the most efficient and effective, but it depends on your needs.

Release

During the last phase of the development cycle, we need to define a way for the world to be able to report a vulnerability. In addition to having a procedure for fixing newly found vulnerabilities, we need an incidence response plan and we need training.

Incidence Response Plan

An incidence response plan outlines the internal and external steps to take in the event of a breach. It describes what should be done and answers a number of internal questions: Who should be contacted? How do we contact them? If we can't reach the primary contacts, who is next on the list? What are the standard operating procedures to be taken for each breach type? Externally, it also answers the question, what should be done? For example, what if a breach is leaked to the press? Not leaked to the press? Who is handling PR? Who defines and controls the message? The incidence response plan is a living document that needs to be practiced in advance of a real breach occurring.

Training

Training consists of training employees on the common human vulnerabilities exploited to gain access. This is called human engineering. Staff must be taught to recognize phishing and spear phishing and the other human exploitative practices hackers use. This is important. It is how hackers access "impenetrable" systems. Training also includes practicing the incidence response plan to flush out any operational issues before they become a problem.

RISK MANAGEMENT AND ASSESSMENT

Risk management is the business counterpart to security. While it should be considered in the context of the SDLC, it's separated here along with privacy to provide more emphasis and detail to these two very important business topics.

It is the responsibility of management to ensure that a process occurs that assesses and then mitigates risk and its associated liabilities. As mentioned earlier, security is not a technical problem; with enough budget we can pay the price to reduce risk to near zero. But that's not practical. You have a finite budget for security, so you must decide on the best way to apply it.

Risk assessment is an exercise in balancing tolerable risk with security costs (see Figure 16.2). The output is a set of engineering priorities and requirements for the model, application, and analytics and an explicit risk profile for executive management. Risk assessment consists of four steps:

1. Take asset (data) inventory.

2. Identify attack vectors.

3. Calculate risks.

4. Balance risks with costs.

Let's go through each of them in more detail.

| Figure 16.2 | **Balancing risks with costs** |

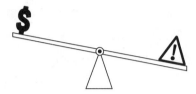

1. Take Asset (Data) Inventory

The first step in risk assessment is to do an audit of your IoT product to compile an inventory of where the data assets live. These assets will be embedded in things, in the fog, and in the cloud. These assets can be in motion or at rest. Data in motion will be shuttled from the sensors and external systems to the software-defined product (application and cybermodel), which can live in the physical product and anywhere else on the network compute fabric. Data will also travel between a consolidated data lake and separate data pools to feed analytics. When the assets are in the data lake and data pools, their vulnerability is the same as any IT data stored in a private or public cloud.

Once completed, your company should have an asset inventory of the location of the data, the nature and purpose of the data, and any legal or regulatory issues to consider for the data. This is performed by engineering.

2. Identify Attack Vectors

The second step in risk assessment is to technically identify where cyberattacks are most likely to occur using a process called threat modeling. The unique attack vectors of your product are identified by looking at cloud security, network security, application security, and mobile security. Since an IoT product is a system of systems, security must be considered at the interface between each system and at the interfaces between people and each system. This is where the vulnerabilities lie. It is these interfaces, where data flow in and out, that must be identified and then protected from cyberattacks. For each identified attack vector, engineering estimates the cost of time and equipment to mitigate it.

3. Calculate Risks

The third step in risk assessment is to step through each of the identified attack vectors, applying the formula:

$$Risk = impact * likelihood$$

The risk associated with each attack vector is the multiplication of the impact and the likelihood, resulting in a value between 0 and 1. This calculation is performed by business and engineering, but ironically it is as much an art as it is a science.

Impact

Impact ultimately represents how much money the company would be liable for if a breach occurred at that attack vector. Instead of dollars, this value is mapped to a number between 0 and 1. Business calculates this by considering the potential legal liability, financial liability, and brand reputation liability associated with the breach.

Likelihood

Likelihood is the probability of a breach occurring. Engineering assigns a number between 0 and 1 by assessing the types of technical threats (confidentiality, integrity, and availability) that can occur for that attack vector.

4. Balance Risks with Costs

The last step in risk assessment is purely a business one. It balances the risk with the cost of developing the cybersecurity necessary to thwart the risk at each attack vector. This process ultimately prioritizes the security requirements to be folded into the overall requirements document for engineering.

This four-step process may sound onerous, but it need not be. The detail and amount of time dedicated to risk assessment is a function of the maximum liability the organization can incur and resources available. Most important is going through the exercise to bubble up a list of priorities at some level of granularity and to then knock them off, one at a time, within the reality of the organization's circumstances.

Example

Let's consider two extreme examples for the IoT BWE. Sensor data streaming from sensor number 4251, representing temperature at one of a hundred joints, have a pretty low impact if the data are read, spoofed, or interrupted. It's probably not worth encrypting, because if a bad actor gets these data, the relative liability is low. If erroneous data are injected or the data are jammed up, again, the relative liability—and "relative" is the operative word—is low. So impact for this attack vector is *low*. Maybe we mistakenly douse the joint with water, or maybe we mistakenly flag it to be examined during the next scheduled maintenance; not so much of a big deal. Given the location and overall purpose of this joint in the grand scheme of things, the motivation, and therefore the likelihood of this happening, is *low*. So together these two factors of low impact and low likelihood, when multiplied out, will be a relatively low number, and as such, places this security requirement near the bottom of our priority list.

On the other hand, let's say bucket wheel excavator operators must authenticate themselves through a web server to start their shift. DDoS attack tools are effective and simple to find and therefore represent a *high* likelihood of attack, because if the goal was to take down this machine, this is a relatively easy way to do it. The impact of such an attack would also be *high*, because without a new crew logging in, the BWE cannot operate. Together, the high likelihood and high impact associated with this attack vector multiplies out to be a relatively high number. Given the high risk, this security requirement would be placed near the top of our priority list to be further prioritized based on mitigation cost.

The login authentication server is at higher risk than sensor 4251, so securing it would place it higher in our security requirements list.

PRIVACY

B2B relationships between the buyer and seller are explicitly laid out and contractually agreed upon by both businesses and are generally vetted by attorneys. B2C relationships are not. This explains why governments worldwide protect their citizen consumers. It's no different for IoT, and since this plays out in the public, we hear about this form of liability (not protecting the privacy of the buyer) more than the others.

Who owns the data from a medical device implanted in a patient? Is it the patient? Or maybe it's the device manufacturer?

Or is it the healthcare provider that implanted the device and is using it to manage the health of the patient?

Well, it turns out that no one owns the data, at least right now in most of the world. The better question to ask is, who has the right to use the data? It's still the Wild Wild West out there regarding data rights, but the best answer is to get a broad contract "signed" assigning your company the data rights from the entity the data originate from. This assignment, however, is still murky, and furthermore, the form of such requests varies, and in some IoT use cases there is no interface that could even request such consent.

In addition to consent, depending on the industry, there may also be regulations and laws to comply with. Most notably in the United States, there is HIPPA for healthcare and the FTC for consumer goods—both dealing directly with how personally identifiable information should be used and protected.

People are concerned about their privacy. Consumers and corporate entities too want to know how their data are being used, if the data are being sold, and if people and companies can be explicitly identified by the data. For the foreseeable future, you need to use common sense to avoid getting into trouble with the authorities. Every situation is contextual, but use reasonable judgment. If you don't do anything false, deceptive, or unfair, you should be fine.

Best Practices

Everyone wants the data. Whereas security is designed to keep the external bad actors away from end-user data, a privacy policy is designed to keep the internal good guys away. These internal policies to guide employees must be developed and enforced. Although policies differ from company to company, a guiding principle is to treat the data how you would like your data to be treated. There are no hard-and-fast rules; just use common sense, be fair, and be ethical. Luckily the following privacy best practices that have proved themselves over the years can be used to guide your internal policies.

Be Transparent

Be clear to the end users about what will happen with their data. Educate them; don't obfuscate the issue in a backhanded attempt to confuse the situation.

Make an Explicit Trade

I have the worst sense of direction and get lost all the time. Even in my town of 80,000 people, I still find myself punching a local address into my phone if I'm running late. I love GPS-based mapping and don't know how I found my way before it turned up on my phone. But these free applications don't come for free. In exchange, the mapping service provider knows exactly where I live, where I go, how long I stay there, and where I shop. And I'm OK with that, because there is an explicit trade in value: my data for the provider's useful service. Offer an explicit trade of value in exchange for data, even if this trade is simply framed by how the IoT product will function with and without the data.

Don't Take More Than You Need

A scatter-gun approach to data collection is wrong on so many levels. As I promote in this book, explicitly identify the data you need to collect. Don't collect more because you believe in the romantic notion that at some point in the future the magic of data science is going to reveal a treasure trove of valuable information you can sell. The likelihood is not worth the cost of gathering and storing the data, nor is it worth the long-term risk of keeping the data. Have a data plan.

Keep Data for as Short a Time as Possible

Related to how much data you keep is how long you keep the data. Transform the data into information as per your plan and get rid of the original data. Again, it's tempting to keep the data for a wished-for payday in the future, but don't; it's not worth the risk. The longer you have the data, the more risk you incur.

The Endgame

Communicate how long you will keep the data and what you will do once you're finished with the data. Establishing a time cap is reassuring for people and companies—they don't want their data out there forever. And be clear on what you will do after you are finished with the data. It is more comforting to consumers and corporations to know that you will delete their data and all backed-up instances of those data, across all your data pools and data lake, than to wonder if their data are going to be eventually sold.

CONCLUSION

Sitting on the back-left corner of my desk are two products covered by a thin layer of dust. Neither has been touched in a long time, and that's not a good sign. They're there not for sentimental reasons; they're there to remind me of two important lessons, both covered in this book.

The dust on my landline handset is understandable. I never use it, and no one of any importance to me ever calls it. The only reason it occupies a permanent place on my desk is by some sorcery that makes my bill cheaper with the landline than without it. It is an example of a traditional product category subsumed by an IoT product, in this case, the original mass produced IoT product: the smartphone.

The bigger problem is the IoT product that sits beside it. If I plug it into the CAN bus of my car, it will tell me all sorts of things that I can't remember right now, but I'm pretty sure it will tell me the history of my car's speed. And that is important to me.

My teenage daughter drives her car way too fast. And since I pay for her car insurance and care deeply about her safety, I should be highly motivated to take a few minutes and install this IoT device. Yet there it sits, collecting dust on my desk, where I've seen it every day for the last 18 months, ever since it was given to me after an IoT presentation I delivered in Las Vegas.

This is a problem—a problem that needs to be solved by everyone developing products in IoT today. If I, who love IoT and make my living from it, can't be bothered to install this free device into the car of my lead-footed daughter, who will?

The problem is that its value doesn't outweigh its cost, which in this case is just my time! Had the manufacturer followed my stringent process of value modeling and then the 360-degree requirements process explained in this book, this product would have never seen the light of day. It would have never failed so miserably, like so many other IoT products before it.

Let's go back and revisit other important lessons to remember from this book.

KEY TECH

An IoT product's power, and value, comes from abstracting its physical IoT functionality into a virtual model that quantifies the product's IoT value proposition. The model and application constitute the software-defined product, and the rest of an IoT product is a data-collecting and -analyzing machine. Data come from their sensors and from external systems, such as data services, business systems, and, most profoundly, other IoT products. The entire product is tied together by the network fabric.

Analytics rounds off the trio of value (the other two being the model and application) and is used, along with the application, to transform the data into useful information—because all incremental value in an IoT product comes from transforming its data into useful information. Value defines what information we need, which defines what data we need to collect, which defines the data-collecting tech we need to integrate together.

THE FOUR WAYS TO VALUE

The first way to create value with IoT is by enabling innovative features that make the product better. Innovation is enabled not only by having more data but by having a built-in way to analyze those data and then transform them into value. Voice control and Internet search are two such IoT features that make the new generation of wireless speakers far superior to their non-IoT counterparts.

The second way is by operating the product better. One of the hottest product categories exemplifying this today is autonomous vehicles. The better operation of cars in the United States alone is projected to save over 30,000 lives per year from traffic fatalities. The government isn't advocating and funding driverless cars because it's cool technology; the government is behind these cars, pushing them along, because in this case IoT saves lives. Operating the product better is also core to improving operational efficiency and IoT picks up from where IT left off.

The third way to create incremental value with IoT is to maintain products better. Predictive maintenance, for example, uses IoT analytics to determine failure before it occurs. This increases asset utilization in a big way.

Last, IoT can create new products . . . better, by fostering invention. This is done by not only listening to customers but quantifying their actions. This leads to new versions and new variations of existing products. But if we listen to and quantify all the data we collect, this can lead to completely new categories of products—and possibly to new markets to sell to. Access to these private data must be explicitly and equitably bargained for before we can fully tap this type of value creation.

TWO PARALLEL PATHS

These are the ways to create value with the Internet of Things, but *how* we create and monetize value takes us down two parallel technology paths, paradoxically leading us to the same place: outcomes.

As IoT products evolve, we will be able to bring more of them together to jointly deliver more of what the customer wants. First, they evolve from smart products to connected products to IoT products. Then IoT products talk to each other within a product line, and eventually they will talk to each other between product lines from different vendors. Standards play an important supporting role, but it is the IoT platform that's the star, for it is the technical underpinning to deliver outcomes.

On the second and parallel path, IoT technology enables our products to measure more of our customers' business models, and in doing so, it evolves the IoT business model from the product business model to the service business model and then ultimately to the outcome business model, which by definition mimics the customer's business model.

Aligning business models aligns business objectives, creating a more intimate customer relationship and a true partnership, one where the vendors do well only when their customers do. It is the IoT ecosystem, the business counterpart to the IoT platform, that monetizes the IoT by combining multiple business models into the one presented to the customer.

OUTCOMES—IOT'S KILLER APP

Individually, IoT products are superior to their traditional counterparts in every imaginable way, but IoT's killer app is outcomes.

Let's face it: your customers don't really want your product; what they want is what it can do for them. Farmers, for example, don't want to own and maintain tractors; what they want is a bumper crop for the lowest possible cost.

But tractors alone can't achieve this, and so leading tractor manufacturers are using the Internet of Things to bring together their tractors with other farming machinery, as well as with irrigation systems, seed management, and weather data, to deliver a higher-yielding crop at a lower cost. And this is sold as an outcome for a percentage of the profits.

Groups of products, all working in concert to deliver the outcome the customer wants, are brought together by the IoT platform and monetized by the IoT ecosystem. And it is the summation of these ecosystems, within specific geographies, that produces the Outcome Economy. This is an economy where outcomes are bought and sold, yielding the trillion-dollar market-size projections typically attributed to the Internet of Things.

PLOTTTING YOUR STRATEGY

The concept of using IoT technology to deliver and effectively monetize outcomes is the key to developing your IoT strategy. Outcomes rewire industries, changing who your competitors and partners are. Your customer may change too, but you can be sure that your company will. To most effectively build, sell, and support an IoT product requires a company transformation. And once a company sees its industry, competition, customers, and operations through the IoT lens, it has the perspective needed to develop its IoT business plan.

THE REAL CHALLENGE

IoT's greatest challenge isn't technical; it's business. Granted, the lack of standardization and strong enough security are big tech challenges, but we can and will solve them. But they won't be solved, nor will IoT get past its hype and its early adopters, until the Internet of Things makes companies more money. This has been the purpose of this book; my hope is that it has given you that different business perspective and some ideas of how to leverage this new tech within your business.

WHAT'S NEXT

Just as the Internet is part of every business, so too will be the Internet of Things—it's a natural technical evolution. The revolution comes from how you choose to use it in your business. Given that IoT is coming, all businesses must plan for it. Now that you have read this book, develop your IoT business plan—you're ready. This will reduce competitive risk and prepare you to decide when to spend the time and the resources needed to leverage the Internet of Things to develop your IoT business and product line.

INDEX

ABOUT THE AUTHOR

Bruce Sinclair started in the business of IoT in 2008 as CEO of a networking company that sold a smart home–enabling platform to Internet service providers. He began his career as a mathematician and then programmer who quickly found his way to business through marketing, and he has been CEO of companies in the visual computing and IT industries.

Today Bruce is the publisher of http://www.iot-inc.com and advises brands, manufacturers and vendors on their IoT strategies, and also keynotes on the Internet of Things at events around the world.

Bruce is known in the industry from his podcast, video series, and monthly meetup in the Silicon Valley, and he is a featured author for leading business and technology publications. He lives in Northern California with his wife and two children.

Find out more about Bruce and his consulting, speaking, courses, and workshops at http://www.brucesinclair.net.

IoT Inc. Workbook

Download the accompanying *IoT Inc. Workbook*, free of charge, at http://www.iot-inc.com/workbook. Matching this book chapter by chapter, this companion document highlights key concepts and links to select podcasts, videos and articles that go into more depth on important topics.

IoT Inc. Buyer's Guide

Specific products and services are not referred to in this book since they change over time. See the latest commercial offers in the *Iot-Inc Buyer's Guide*, found at http://www.iot-inc.com/buyers-guide.

IoT Inc. Online Courses

A series of online courses based on this book can be found at, http://www.iot-inc.com/online-courses.